I0008092

Design Patterns
of
Catholic God

CHURCH DOCTRINE
IN SOFTWARE TERMS
WITHOUT
SIMPLIFICATION AND PREJUDICE

Karel Moulik

About the Book

Imagine understanding Catholic doctrine like a pro after reading a single, average-sized book written in terms you already know.

This book presents the Catholic faith through clear and accurate software analogies, preserving its inner logic and beauty without dumbing it down.

It also offers a compact, contemporary thought model for practical reasoning, much like the thought models understood by ordinary people in the Middle Ages.

If you have some experience in software development, you can easily grasp the precise version of what Catholics believe and why—without needing prior knowledge of biblical terminology or the centuries-old philosophy of Aristotle and Aquinas.

To believe or not? You can make an informed choice.

This book is free of culture-war rhetoric.

Your feedback is invaluable! If you have suggestions for improvement or topics you would like to see explored further, please email designpatterns@karelmoulik.com.

Acknowledgements

I want to thank my lawyer friend, Tomas Hromek, for the endless, fiery conversations we have had over the years. He is the one who always knows the correct answers, yet we struggled immensely to put into words the reasoning of the Church behind them in a way that holds precise meaning and remains understandable to both of us today. Our conversation is far from over—we have yet to reach a settlement—but without him, this book would never have seen the light of day.

Copyright ©2025 Karel Moulik. All Rights Reserved.

You are encouraged to quote passages from this book in reviews, articles, essays, books, and other works, provided that proper attribution is given. However, reproducing full chapters or more than 10 percent of the book without written permission is prohibited.

For permissions beyond brief excerpts, please contact:
designpatterns@karelmoulik.com

ISBN (paperback): 979-8-314-95545-1
Published by **Biorg s.r.o.** (based in Czechia, EU)

Scripture Quotations:

Bible quotations in this book are marked with a version-specific suffix. The following attributions correspond to their respective suffixes.

NIV *(104 verses)*: The Holy Bible, New International Version®, NIV® Copyright ©1973, 1978, 1984, 2011 by Biblica, Inc.®
Used by permission. All rights reserved worldwide.
ISV *(19 verses)*: The Holy Bible: International Standard Version. Release 2.0, Build 2015.02.09. Copyright ©1995-2014 by ISV Foundation. ALL RIGHTS RESERVED INTERNATIONALLY.
Used by permission of Davidson Press, LLC.
ESV *(12 verses)*: Scripture quotations are from The ESV®Bible
(The Holy Bible, English Standard Version®), ©2001 by Crossway, a publishing ministry of Good News Publishers.
Used by permission. All rights reserved.
CEB *(5 verses)*: Scripture quotations from the COMMON ENGLISH BIBLE. ©Copyright 2011 COMMON ENGLISH BIBLE. All rights reserved.
Used by permission. (www.CommonEnglishBible.com).
KJ21 *(4 verses)*: Scripture quotations taken from the 21st Century King James Version®, copyright ©1994. Used by permission of Deuel Enterprises, Inc., Gary, SD 57237. All rights reserved.
AMP, AMPC *(2 verses)*: Scripture quotations taken from the Amplified®Bible (AMP), Copyright ©2015
by The Lockman Foundation. Used by permission. lockman.org
NLT *(1 verse)*: Scripture quotations marked NLT are taken from the Holy Bible, New Living Translation, copyright ©1996, 2004, 2015 by Tyndale House Foundation. Used by permission of Tyndale House Publishers, Inc., Carol Stream, Illinois 60188.
All rights reserved.

Quotations from Introduction to Christianity by Joseph Ratzinger:
All translations from the original German to English were done
by Karel Moulik, the author of this book.

All quotations, except those from the Preface to the 2000 edition, were
translated based on: Ratzinger, J. (1972). Einführung in das Christentum:
Vorlesungen über das apostolische Glaubensbekenntnis. Kösel.
(ISBN: 978-3423040945)

All quotations from the Preface to the 2000 edition were translated based on:
Ratzinger, J. (2000). Einführung in das Christentum: Vorlesungen über das
apostolische Glaubensbekenntnis (New ed.). Kösel.
(ISBN: 978-3466204557)

Quotations Marked CCC:
All quotations from the Compendium
of the Catechism of the Catholic Church were taken from:
https://www.vatican.va/archive/compendium_ccc/documents/archive_2005_compendium-ccc_en.html

Quotations of the Creed:
The text of the Creed was taken from USCCB:
https://www.usccb.org/beliefs-and-teachings/what-we-believe

Cover Page Image:
The book cover was designed by Karel Moulik, the author.
The image used was sourced from freely available NASA images:
https://earthobservatory.nasa.gov/images/885/earth-from-space

Dedicated to my dear friend Marek Sebesta, a scientist deeply knowledgeable in chemistry, biology, music, philosophy, history, and culture—yet who, remarkably, has never encountered this story in a truly acceptable form.

Contents

Part I

Reason's Path to God

— 1 —

Core Message

As I write these lines in the midst of 2024, people are fascinated by the achievements and promises of information technology (IT). Over the past two decades, everybody has started using software for almost any activity. While it has revolutionized how we live and solve problems, it is still a relatively new phenomenon and hasn't been around long enough to shape our understanding of God.

In 2024, the notion that humanity's engagement with software development could carry profound theological implications may seem far-fetched. To many, it sounds like a joke. However, no one doubts that the previous eras of Enlightenment and the Industrial Revolution significantly influenced our views on transcendent matters and, more importantly, reshaped how we live and act in this area. The newly developed methods of discovering the truth about the world, which have brought us countless benefits, have also led to confusion among believers and theologians. They have also undoubtedly contributed to a significant brain drain from the Church. As a result, we find ourselves in a crisis over how to think and speak about God.

Nowadays, high school students who excel in math and science might choose to study quantum computing or theoretical physics. Meanwhile, their peers who find these subjects challenging but have a passion for the humanities might turn to theology. Yet, if God exists, aren't the laws of physics just a piece of the puzzle needed to grasp even a fraction of His nature? Sometimes, I fantasize about how theoretical physics would look like if nurtured with the same accents as theology for the past 500 years.

Bishop Robert Barron's motto, "Stop dumbing down the faith," resonates deeply with me. I believe this is a critical step in getting the Church back on track. While philosophers awed by the power of science may easily end up concluding that "God is dead," as a software engineer, I aim to demonstrate in this book that applying concepts, principles, and insights from software design can lead us to an equally natural conclusion that God is the most logical explanation for all things transcendent. And by God, I specifically mean the Catholic God.

There are still too few people with sufficient software design experience to match humanity's needs. Still, the number of them is growing rapidly as more and more people find themselves somehow working in the field of information technology, which necessitates grasping at least some basic software design concepts. I hope these concepts will soon become part of basic literacy. When that happens, we will no longer say we *somehow partially work in the IT field,* just as we don't consider ourselves scribes or mathematicians simply because we fill out tax forms or calculate mortgage payments. When that day comes, I hope this book will be renamed Catholic God for Everyone.

— 2 —

Intended Audience

Before we delve into the subject matter—where the personal 'I' of the author will largely stay in the background—allow me to share a few words about who I am and how this book came to be. I believe this is the most effective way to convey who this book is for. It's written for those who have encountered similar challenges and made similar mistakes at various points in their lives. At the same time, it's also for anyone who is entirely unlike me—those who have never viewed faith from a similar perspective.

I was baptized into the Catholic Church a few weeks after my birth, but my parents did not honor the promise they made to God during the ceremony: To raise me in the faith. They never spoke of faith at home, as they were unaware of its meaning. I grew up atheist and discovered my baptism only by chance many years later. This revelation came when I was dealing with official paperwork for the first time on my own. Nervous and inexperienced, I accidentally mistook my baptismal certificate for my birth certificate. In my native language, 'first name' literally translates as 'baptismal name,' so it felt natural to assume that a birth certificate might be called a 'baptismal certificate.' This embarrassing mix-up, compounded by my anxiety about navigating the bureaucratic process, remains a vivid memory.

For those born into Catholic families, this story may seem barely believable. I share it to illustrate the profound divide that exists in some parts of the world between the religious and non-religious spheres of society. This unexpected discovery made me a rather weird kind of Catholic, and I suspect I still am one, albeit for different reasons.

Around the same time, I also began questioning the coherence of the worldview that had been presented to me by those around me. In this sense, learning about my baptism was surprisingly helpful.

All my objections to the prevailing worldview were entirely rational. There was no trace of mysticism in my life back then. When I subsequently read the Gospels, I began appreciating them strictly from a rational point of view. They described the workings of my personal experience so precisely that I came to see them as analogous to the physical laws governing the natural world—only applied to the inner life.

Having already been baptized, my discovery of the Gospels did not push me even an inch closer to any religious community. For many years, I remained in this state. I felt I belonged to Christ, yet I was completely unaware of the Catholic tradition. I viewed the Catholic Church as a bastion of traditionalism and prescientific customs, a world where rational thinkers like myself would find little welcome.

Whenever I listened to clergy or believers being vocal in public, their interpretations of the Gospels seemed oversimplified, to the point where the message itself appeared lost. They used unfathomable phrases and when asked for clarification, they offered poetic analogies that only muddled things further.

Some spoke in a condescending tone, suggesting that believers should simply accept the words as they are rather than trying to understand them. They argued that true understanding was impossible and that any attempt to seek it was a sign of pride.

On the other hand, some of those I encountered were very open-minded, embracing any viewpoint, even those that seemed almost completely at odds with the internal logic of the Gospels. It was their belief that we should all be kind to one another and not take the pursuit of truth in its complexity too seriously, as doing so would be a sign of pride.

But wrestling with one's lack of understanding of the world is no sign of pride. However, despising such efforts—or assuming that the battle has already been won in a way that one cannot comprehend—seemed to me a manifestation of pride for sure. To me, these two approaches differed only in their tone of speech, and they left me skeptical and suspicious of the corresponding forms of faith that seemed to me as little more than an empty custom.

I felt repelled by the Church's public image. Filled with sadness at the thought that I might never experience a community of like-minded

Christians, I turned inward, immersing myself in the philosophical writings of thinkers such as Descartes, Pascal, and Kant. These works offered little about the sacramental life but plenty of fascinating discussions about the laws of the universe, where God was deeply integrated into the picture. This led me to an intellectual enthusiasm for reconciling two perspectives: The scientific worldview, often presented in popular, aggressively atheistic books, and the remarkably accurate model of inner life I found in the Gospels. Both seemed equally true and elegant to me.

When I was eighteen, I even authored a short book on this topic, though I never attempted to publish it. Since then, I've never doubted that these two views—one grounded in science, the other in faith—can be harmoniously combined. Now, 22 years later, I remain passionate about this challenge. Many of the ideas I had back then have found their way into this text. Yet today, I am almost certain that these two worlds cannot be bridged without an understanding of the sacramental life within a community, without addressing Church tradition, and without an honest discussion of how we arrived at our current cultural and spiritual condition.

My first encounter with my 'everyday' Catholic neighbors took place around the time of my wedding. Since a civil marriage was not acceptable to me, I needed to approach the parish where we lived at the time. There, I quickly realized that my faith and views on the Gospel aligned well with those of my 'everyday' Catholic neighbors. They were genuinely willing to take the Gospels seriously and search for the complex truth—an endeavor that, like exploring the field of physics and any other field of science, is always humbling and filled with inherent uncertainty.

Some time later, I completed my preparation for the Sacrament of Confirmation, was confirmed, and received my First Communion. Although I was now in full communion with the Church, I still felt estranged from its hierarchy and public image—a sentiment that is not uncommon among my 'everyday' Catholic neighbors.

As time went on and my faith deepened—not only intellectually but also in every aspect of my life—I began to wonder: Were the sincere, thoughtful Catholics I knew personally outliers, or was it the Church hierarchy and the loudest voices on both the left and right that represented some kind of strange aberration?

Surprisingly, what helped me resolve this question wasn't a particular book I read or a personal encounter. Instead, it was something unexpected: The TV series by Bishop Robert Barron, called Catholicism. While watching this visually and intellectually rich masterpiece, I had a striking realization: This is me—this has been me all along, ever since I first read the Gospels. I don't live in the Church of the last 200, 100, or even 50 years—I live in the Church of the past 2000 years. That is where I belong and where I truly feel at home.

I do not live in a starving, old-fashioned, besieged fortress. Instead, I am part of a mighty river of immense power—a force that sometimes flows beneath the surface of the Earth, hidden from view, only to emerge once again, carving rocks, cutting edges, and surging to the surface with unstoppable strength.

The following may sound a bit awkward at this point, but by the time you've finished reading this book, it will make perfect sense: I believe that advances in information technology, computer science, and the tensions between classical and quantum physics are all like knocks on the door—and it is the Lord Jesus who is knocking.

If any part of my story resonates with you, then I wrote this book for you.

— 3 —

Objective

I'm a software engineer, not a learned theologian, yet this book is about God and the Catholic faith. If I wrote a well-crafted collection of beliefs and personal opinions intertwined with my personal story, it would hold the same relevance as other similar books. In my case, the relevance would be zero, and my effort would only reinforce the general notion that the Catholic faith is merely a wise set of recommendations for living a good life, another competitor among many systems of habits, beliefs, and practices. Dressed in a new, eloquent, and elegant way, I could describe a system that worked best for me, which I now offer as a recipe to others on how to live.

No! It causes me physical pain even to write a characterization like this. I have no interest in creating yet another self-help guide filled with personal anecdotes, mental exercises, or dietary advice. As a software engineer, I'm primarily interested in design—which means the world's design in this context. And I appreciate you may have good reasons to believe this world was not designed by anyone—we will get to that. The point I want to make for now is that times have changed, and with sufficient funding, for the first time in human history, you can sit in front of your computer and become a creative designer of another world. It will undoubtedly be an infinitely less perfect and beautiful world than the real one, but that doesn't mean we can't discuss the fundamental design decisions to be made in that process.

Some of these design concerns will also apply to the real world if we later entertain the possibility that it didn't get its current shape and form by pure accident, but rather for a reason, by a reason. Our findings about the design of the world may prove to be as hard as rock, as solid

10

as the design patterns discovered by science. They may often apply on the personal level—if we analyze a world design livable from the 'first-person view'—but they may not be subjective at all. I recall reading the "Discourse on the Method" by René Descartes in high school. I still admire the ethos of this book of building knowledge solely on findings that are beyond doubt. I admire how this way of thinking later ignited scientific exploration on a never-seen-before scale.

I see this exploration as a *reverse engineering of the real world from its machine code up.* The discoveries were indeed stunning, yet certain higher-level concepts may become nearly invisible when you *hack the matter from the atomic level up.* In this way, it's no different from hacking compiled binaries in the hope you later infer the high-level architecture diagram. Thus, in keeping with the Cartesian ethos, I plan to employ a top-down approach in this book. As we've discussed, it's no sci-fi anymore, at least not for software engineers.

At the beginning of his book Introduction to Christianity, Joseph Ratzinger describes with sadness how, in the nineteenth century, it became the general opinion that the Catholic religion belonged to the subjective, private realm and should have its place there. Indeed, we will conduct our exploration mainly within these same borders.

Ratzinger asks:

> Has not the Christian consciousness largely—without realizing it—come to terms with the idea that faith in God is something subjective, belonging to the private sphere rather than to the shared activities of public life, in which people have had to organize themselves, in order to cooperate, "etsi Deus non daretur" (as if God did not exist)?

Although this description might still accurately reflect reality today, I hope that the situation it describes is no longer beyond reconciliation. But we must approach the Catholic faith as a genuine pursuit of truth rather than merely as a collection of wise practices, exercises, dietary recommendations, and traditional festivities to make your life (and afterlife) more livable.

If seeking the truth becomes secondary to pursuing the practical promises of your faith—even salvation itself—you will inevitably confine your faith to the private realm, merely as a system of your private choice.

What's worse, in your eyes, proponents of such a system will become the exalted custodians of wisdom rather than your fellow researchers with whom you tread the same path. Ultimately, you will lose your faith. It's trivial: No matter how much you fight with yourself (and others) to resuscitate it in your heart, you can never truly believe anything you didn't discover through a genuine quest for truth (besides perhaps some basic self-evident truths).

Certainly, you must learn from authorities, but you can never outsource your search for truth to any exalted custodians of wisdom. Instead, you need to be like a humble and critical scientist—just not out there in the Newtonian space but rather inside, from the first-person view of your soul.

There may be experts in physics or Catholic doctrine, but when it comes to your own life, you are the only true expert who possesses all the relevant facts and bears full responsibility for doing what is right. Delegating such a quest for truth to *more competent* superiors has led to all of the worst abominations of the past. For many contemporary Catholics, who call themselves 'lay people,' this attitude often manifests as an unhealthy reverence for certain theologians whom they view with awe as wise men rather than analogous to competent senior researchers. Even more troubling is how easily this same tendency causes laypeople to idolize their favorite priests, elevating them to the status of gurus. And I'm afraid we are unwittingly drawn to gurus only to be abused, and conversely, we ourselves become gurus to abuse others—sometimes unwittingly.

I write this book as a mere fellow researcher—not from any position of authority, formal or informal. I'm as far from a guru as one can be. I also don't intend to bring any new doctrinal findings here since everything on the subject has already been described very well in the past. The problem with these explanations is that they can only be adequately understood after you become familiar with the Catholic terminology and the Biblical story, which requires a significant effort rarely invested without having at least a suspicion that you ought to put God above everything else in your life. This entry barrier is what this book will try to erode. You may find new ways to explain the basic concepts and some new observations here, but otherwise, read it as you would read a book on physics—certainly not to learn the author's personal opinion on life in space.

To double down on this intention, let me also reveal the ancient genre of this book. De facto, you are reading a commentary on the work of a renowned author, namely on the already mentioned Introduction to Christianity by Joseph Ratzinger. When I read his book for the first time, it occurred to me how close his way of thinking was to the mind of a software engineer. I will try to translate some of what he says into how a software engineer would put it.

I am a Catholic. While many of the concepts discussed in this book may be relevant to all of Christianity—not just Catholicism—I will focus exclusively on the context of the Catholic faith. This is because I am not an expert on the differences between Christian denominations. I believe it would be misguided to limit discussions about God—whom we all share—to only those with specialized religious expertise.

— 4 —

Basic Terms

Allow me to briefly clarify some key terms you will encounter throughout this book.

Seeking Truth: In the following few chapters, we will initially focus on the quest for truth rather than on God. This approach is based on everyone's universal, firsthand experience—we have all encountered situations where we fought notions that were demonstrably not true. Although defining truth can be complex—and perhaps even impossible—its existence is undeniable. Or at least, very few of us would argue that truth is a completely void concept at all levels.

Being Faithful: Faith is the act of remaining faithful. You can be faithful to traditions, your ancestors, or a way of life. For Catholic Christians, God and truth are one and the same. That is why, throughout this book, whenever we speak of having faith or being faithful, we are referring to prioritizing the pursuit of truth above all else in our lives. If we are not faithful to the truth, if we lack faith, it suggests that we have placed something else—such as happiness or self-esteem—on a higher pedestal. When we later discuss God, the meaning of faith or being faithful will retain the same essence.

Belief: Similarly, a belief is our decision to regard something as true. While we may hope for certainty in the future, in most cases, it can be proven beyond a reasonable doubt that no certainty will ever be given to us. As a result, our decision to believe is always provisional, based on the evidence available at the time, which can later be challenged or refuted by new findings. Even in mathematics and logic, we depend on the belief that our reasoning and calculations are free from errors.

Fanaticism: Efforts to cement our beliefs as unchangeable—no matter how sincere and thorough our previous quest for truth was—are attempts to fall into fanaticism. Fanaticism represents a state of uncertainty deliberately kept out of our consciousness. The distinction between being fanatic about something and holding a belief lies in our willingness to reassess our stance based on new evidence, welcoming it whenever it may come. Fanatics put a false, self-imposed sense of certainty above everything else, making it impossible for them—by definition—to be faithful at the same time.

— 5 —

Point of Origin

When you are born, you enter this world with an instinct to discover essential truths about how things work here. Despite all the love and care from your parents, you will not survive long if you can't learn at least some basic laws of physics concerning gravity, heat, or kinetic energy. You are like a little scientist conducting your own private baby research.

Of course, you don't discover these laws for society as a whole but rather for your private understanding. On the other hand, it has everything a genuine research should have: You must be ready to suppress your ego and accept the truth no matter what you wish it to be or what your current experience tells you. At the beginning of your life, you either uphold the ethos of a true scientist or you fail, and it's all over.

Initially, you start life much like an alien attempting to settle on an unknown planet. Fortunately, your parents will lovingly and mercifully lend you enough time to learn the fundamental truths. Still, you are born with a debt of not knowing the essential truths.

Later, you grow up, become an adult, and no longer feel alien to this planet. You have settled successfully and are no longer in the business of doing your private baby research, upholding the ethos of a true scientist. The question is: Why?

Do you now possess these fundamental truths? If not, what falsely contented you and made you so comfortable you no longer feel the painful debt of not knowing the truth? And here I mean the truth of your particular life situation on the personal level that you used to earn via your private baby-like research rather than the *cardinal secret truths about the universe* we can all read in any book of wisdom. The real reason for your satisfaction is that you learned to do things as they have always been done, and you see it works. What a precious achievement!

But consider that in the past, there were times when people sacrificed their firstborns to pagan gods, and it was considered a well-established tradition; it just worked. There have been thousands of similar examples of various severity in any human society.

In the Bible, the terms 'debt' and 'sin' are interchangeable—in Hebrew, it's one word. This false sense of comfort, provided to you by your parents, society, and cultural background, comes from what is referred to as the Original Sin in Catholic terminology—your inherited debt to the truth. Ratzinger describes this concept in similar terms in the chapter "The Individual and the Whole."

Now, if we are meant to be ready to suppress our egos and accept the truth no matter what we wish it to be or what our current experience tells us, the question arises: Where did this ethos of a genuine scientist come from? It certainly didn't originate from babies, not even from Isaac Newton or René Descartes.

In his book, Ratzinger critiques Descartes for his failure to recognize that no one starts as a blank slate—without inherited delusions—which renders his method inadequate for anything beyond the realm of science. He writes:

> To be human is to be a fellow in all dimensions of existence—not only in the present moment, but in such a way that, in each person, the past and future of humanity are also present. Taken together, they appear more and more as a single 'Adam' the closer we look.

Beginning with Adam, the first man, Original Sin is what we collectively pass down to our children. Humanity, as a 'collective Adam,' only worsens this condition unless, on the individual level, each of us can examine what we live in from the perspective of a child seeking the truth.

This appeal for private-realm scientific baby-like research is much older; you can strongly feel the same motivation from the medieval works of St. Thomas Aquinas, arguably the greatest theologian of all time. However, its origins are traced back even further.

In the New Testament of the Bible, there is a chapter about sin, and this is how Jesus opens the chapter:

³ Then he said, "I tell you the truth,
    unless you turn from your sins
    and become like little children,
    you will never get into the Kingdom of Heaven."

Mt 18:3 (NLT)

The most groundbreaking pioneers of science dared to probe the world through the eyes of vulnerable, meek little children. And I have also witnessed this same quality many times in many Catholic men and women who take the words of the Lord Jesus to heart.

— 6 —

Suffering and Contingency

I know many people who believe that seeking truth—whether in science, theology, history, or other fields—is a complete waste of time. It would be really condescending to dismiss their views outright and move on. After all, they could be right. In his book, Joseph Ratzinger provides an example of one of the most consequential saints, Thérèse of Lisieux, shortly before her death:

> She says, for instance, "The ways of reasoning of the worst materialists force themselves upon me." Her mind is besieged by all the arguments against faith; the feeling of faith seems to have vanished, and she now experiences herself as being "in the skin of sinners."

Anyone who strives to live rightly and seek truth will, at some point, experience doubt and despair. This is not due to a lack of evidence for God's existence. Even if the world were designed in such a way that God's presence was undeniable, I admit that in my lowest moments, I would still question His will, especially if His *project* was similar to what it appears to be in this reality of ours. At times, I even find myself suspecting that He deliberately delays *happy endings*, despite the fact that even I can see a clear path to them. This is obviously wrong, and while you may never hear a guru admit such a weakness, don't be fooled by their confident voices. As Ratzinger extensively demonstrates in the chapter "Belief in the World Today," the positions of believers and nonbelievers are closer than many might think.

Before embarking on a journey to explore the world's design from the top down, I believe it is important to first discuss why this endeavor may be worthwhile. In my view, it has much to do with suffering and contingency, which are everyday aspects of our lives.

Many people argue they care about how things truly are, only to the extent that their needs are satisfied. They would argue the chivalrous attitude toward the truth outlined in the previous chapter would only bring them suffering. This perspective is not without merit since it is hard to avoid conflicts and suffering after you become aware of the lies and delusions your parents live in, your country, or your culture.

I was born in 1984 in a country tainted by Russian occupation, which we finally shook off around 1989. The culture they sought to impose on us was so alien that, once we were free, our recovery was swift. Yet even now, 35 years later, deep scars remain in many people's hearts—no matter how hard they try to conceal them. If you bear these scars, people notice. If you don't, they notice that too—and they make sure you feel it.

I often wonder how the first Christians—hunted, persecuted, and killed across the Roman Empire—managed to survive when it was so easy to identify a faithful Christian. Sometimes, the mere tone of your voice is enough to expose you or certain things you don't do. Often, these are small details. You don't need to feel even a bit morally superior to others; they will still sense that something is off about you. In my country, this once provoked wrath; in other societies, it might even land you in prison.

Every nation tends to protect its way of life, including widely shared misconceptions—its inherited debt to the truth, stemming from Original Sin. Every cultural group exhibits this tendency—including religious communities, even the Church itself (while the forgiveness of Original Sin requires acknowledgment, repentance, and a commitment to resist its effects, it does not immediately erase the marks left by its consequences).

Many people fall in line to avoid the suffering of an outcast, trading their pursuit of truth for acceptance and having some of their needs adequately catered for by the group. They may describe themselves as patriots or defenders of traditional values, and many are willing to fight, endure great suffering, or even sacrifice their lives to live like this. They do it to save the status quo and keep the truth safely at bay. It is primarily here where we encounter fanaticism. In Catholic terms, we would say this is what makes us kill the Lord Jesus again and again every single day. However, the question remains: Is trading conformity for truth a worthwhile bargain, and is it even a realistic one?

As little children, we are entirely at the mercy of our parents, and in most cases, we are welcomed into this world with love and care. As we grow and gain independence, we still find ourselves largely at the mercy of the society we live in. In the past, too much non-conformity often meant a certain death, and it remains a harsh reality in many parts of the world today. Conversely, if we manage to blend in without drawing too much attention, we are often treated with love and care within our community and receive some protection against the unpredictable dangers that often arise at random.

It is almost obvious that in any group of people, an accurate understanding of how the world works underpins the ability to provide everyone with love and care. With love and care—not with the abundance of wealth. Here, it is clearly the shared truths, not the commonly held delusions, that facilitate this.

One must ask why, then, do we so often side with the group rather than with truth, even though it is clearly truth that nurtures us and makes us loved, albeit indirectly, through the means of society. Perhaps we lack the eyes of little children, who see everything as if for the first time—like true scientists, unburdened by preconceived notions. As a 'baby researcher' might put it: On this still somewhat unfamiliar planet, you are cared for with love most of the time throughout your life, and the more, the closer you get to the rule of truth. It almost seems as if the planet was designed that way; however, it can also be a pure coincidence. It is up to you to decide what you believe.

There may be a more substantial reason for siding with the group rather than the truth. Notice how oddly the previous sentence sounds! How can one side with something as abstract as 'truth'? A group always consists of people, and relationships exist between you and them. You can side with them or oppose them, but you can hardly compare this to a relationship with something as sterile as 'truth.' Aren't we falling now again into the position of worshippers of some system of practices, habits, and dietary recommendations? It seems like an intricate play with words to say we should relate to the truth since many could argue that truth is not a person. We are simply not internally wired to put a *database of facts* on a pedestal and love it above everything else. If we were designed by someone, we were surely not designed that way.

We were created to live in relationships with other people—with our 'neighbors,' as the Catholic term would be.

I believe we may have just touched on the most consequential design decision in creating this world—assuming, prematurely, that it was designed—and we may have broached it a bit too early in this book. Nevertheless, I must at least offer you a hint now. In the chapter on faith, Ratzinger compares various world religions—Jewish, Roman, and others—and he points out that none of them is centered on belief in truth as such. He writes:

> The [Jewish] Old Testament as a whole did not describe itself under the concept of 'faith' but rather under the concept of 'law.' It is primarily a way of life in which, however, the act of faith gradually gains increasing significance.

> Roman religiosity, on the other hand, primarily understood 'religio' as the observance of certain ritual forms and customs. For them, no act of faith in the supernatural was necessary; such faith could even be entirely absent without one being unfaithful to this religion. What was essential was a system of rites, and their careful observance was what truly mattered.

Ratzinger further writes:

> Buddha—in this, incidentally, comparable to Socrates—points away from himself: It is not his person that matters, but only the path he has shown. Whoever finds the path may forget Buddha.

> But with Jesus, it is precisely his person, himself, that matters. (...) The path consists precisely in following him, for "I am the way, the truth, and the life" (John 14:6).

Later Ratzinger concludes his chapter on faith:

> Christian faith lives from the fact that there is not only objective meaning, but that this meaning knows and loves me—so that I can lovingly abandon myself to it, with the simplicity

of a child who knows that all its questions are safe in the 'you' of its mother.

To summarize, for a Catholic, truth is a person, and belief in truth is, in essence, a relationship with that person—the Lord Jesus, the living God. Without this pillar, the design of the world would crumble. But we will get to that later. Let's set that aside for now and consider truth as if it were something abstract.

All right. So you might think that seeking the truth is too abstract and not worth risking your comfortable life or jeopardizing the satisfaction of your needs. We could call it the problem of suffering—you suffer when you lack what you need. Today, it's popular to believe that it's almost a human right not to suffer, although it's unclear who granted us this right. The entire political left prioritizes the reduction of suffering in their agenda; it is very humanistic. In Asia, entire religious systems seek to eliminate suffering by reducing attachment to worldly things. Journalists often ask Christians whether their faith helps them suffer less, or what their *recipe* is. Indeed, suffering is evil.

However, this raises an important question: Will prioritizing the elimination of suffering over the pursuit of truth ultimately lead to even greater suffering in the long run? I've observed this firsthand many times, usually in the form of a pursuit of happiness. Let's illustrate this with the example of John:

John always felt that he was just a few steps away from achieving full happiness. First, he needed a good job. After securing one, he wanted a new car, a better house, a holiday, and eventually, a divorce. But even then, he wasn't satisfied. He needed more money, as his car no longer met his needs, his house seemed too small and not in a desirable neighborhood, and his new life partner also fell short of his expectations. He found himself working around the clock, launching himself into yet another cycle of his pursuit of happiness to eliminate his suffering. Again, he needed a better job.

People like John suffer immensely in their attempts to eliminate suffering. They often die unhappy, never reaching their desired state of happiness. And even if they do, they die after suffering the consequences of overindulgence—since the human body cannot sustain an infinite intake of everything indefinitely.

On the other hand, I know people with modest and reasonable expectations, unlike John. Their suffering was eventually rewarded with moments of happiness. However, they soon began to suffer again—not from deprivation, but from the fear of losing their joy due to life's inherent uncertainties.

They started insuring themselves against accidents, bad luck, black swan events, and natural disasters, yet they suffered greatly whenever they realized that no insurance could ever be completely foolproof. The future's inherent contingency still loomed over them like the sword of Damocles.

In some cases, family members pitied these men and women for their suffering and devoted much time and effort to help. Yet contingency can never be fully eliminated. I know of cases firsthand where people came close. But then it rained. Or flights got canceled. For those accustomed to living in a perfectly insured state of joy, even minor disruptions—in a few years—led to nervous breakdowns, a gradual reliance on psychopharmaceuticals, hospitalization, and eventually, death.

To summarize, even if truth were entirely abstract, seeking it might still be preferable to focusing primarily on eliminating suffering. If the people we discussed had concentrated on doing what is right and doing it well—an outcome that naturally follows from pursuing truth—they might not have achieved constant happiness or avoided suffering. But they would have likely attained inner peace. And maybe that is what they truly wanted all along.

— 7 —

Matter in Itself

In this chapter, we will use software design as an analogy to help us understand the design of the world. This is purely an analogy; I do not imply that we live in a simulated environment or that God is an engineer—though, interestingly, Jesus was one. Analogies are frequently used in physics. For example, we describe light as either particles or waves, even though it is fundamentally neither. We model light as particles or waves in calculations, such as scripts for determining parameters of a device that will utilize light for some ends, because these models provide the best practical results.

Even though many people believe that *light is actually photons*, as software engineers, we clearly understand that this is nonsense because a significant part of our everyday job involves representing real-world objects in a logical universe. For instance, an ancient document can be modeled as a logical entity with attributes such as name, date of creation, and author. This logical model bears far less resemblance to the actual piece of parchment it represents than light does to photons. However, when calculating a histogram of creation dates, it is far more practical to manipulate these logical entities than to work directly with the physical documents. Additionally, we are not just fluent at representing physical objects in logical universes but also all other conceptual analogies in various forms, encompassing anything that can be thought in the mind. These representations can include words, equations, geometric shapes, emotions, music, colors, and more. Complex software frameworks are continually developed to capture and simulate how these things interact and function.

A software framework describing human emotions under various conditions is unlikely to cause unwanted annoyance just because it involves no particles, waves, or other physical phenomena. Unfortunately, the same cannot be said for Catholic doctrine, which is also a logical framework that addresses other things than purely physical phenomena. Unlike the average person today, the statement *light is actually not photons* would most likely not provoke an explosion of anger among software engineers, which, in my opinion, makes software engineers particularly well-suited for theological study. In a sense, we share much in common with medieval thinkers, when theology was at its peak. As Joseph Ratzinger writes in his book:

> For the Ancient and Medieval periods, being itself is true, meaning it is knowable and apprehensible, because God, the intellect par excellence, made it—and He made it by thinking it. For the creative primordial spirit, the Creator Spiritus, thinking and making are one. His thinking is an act of creation. Things exist because they are thought. From the ancient and medieval perspective, therefore, all being is 'thought-being,' the thought of the absolute spirit. This means, conversely, that since all being is thought, all being also has meaning—'Logos,' truth. Human thought, from this perspective, is the afterthought of 'thought-being' itself, the reflection of the thought that is Being itself. Man can rethink the Logos, the meaning of being, because his own Logos, his own reason, is the Logos of the one Logos, the thought of the original thought of the primordial Creator Spiritus who pervades all being.

I say this partially for your amusement, but try rereading the previous paragraph, replacing every instance of 'thinking/thought/logos' with 'coding/code/code.'

In the previous chapter, we concluded that some people would do better if they focused on understanding truth and doing things right, rather than prioritizing the elimination of suffering and contingency in their lives. In software engineering, a similar mistake is often replicated in the logical universe, and this analogy will help us better understand what truth means.

When designing a solution for a given task, a software engineer typically works with a set of functional requirements that must be met. Even if the task is complex, a trained software engineer can code a solution. What distinguishes a good programmer from a bad one is not merely knowing *how it should work*, but truly understanding the matter in itself.

A bad programmer responds to complex requirements with equally complex code, then writes additional—often even more complex—code to handle contingencies (anything that might go wrong). While this approach may seem to enhance software stability, it often results in code that is difficult to understand, review, modify, and maintain. In most cases, this state becomes irrecoverable—the complexity can grow so overwhelming that the code must eventually be discarded entirely. The only question is when.

A good programmer produces code that gives you satisfaction from just reading it. You suddenly understand things as they truly are. Such code is so beautiful and elegant that it gives you peace of mind—despite lacking excessive contingency handling. Any code can fail, but with this code, you feel certain that it would fail only in situations where any alternative code would also fail. You are almost sure to find the same code in its place 10 years from now; it could be there forever.

Understanding truth goes beyond knowing how to achieve things or how they work; it's about understanding the matter in itself. But these are just words. Fortunately, every software engineer has lived through this experience and understands exactly what I mean. It may be very comparable to rethinking/recoding something once elegantly thought in the mind of God, a medieval thinker might add. However, in 1968, Joseph Ratzinger was deeply pessimistic that we would ever again see truth with these eyes. He wrote:

> For our today's scientifically determined attitude, which unwittingly shapes our sense of existence and assigns us a place in the real world, it is characteristic that it is limited to the 'phainomena,' to the apparent and graspable. We have given up searching for the hidden 'in-itselfness' of things, probing into the essence of being itself. Doing so seems to us a fruitless attempt, and the depths of the 'in-itselfness' of being appear ultimately out of reach.

In his chapter about belief, Ratzinger extensively discusses the unfortunate shift from seeking to understand the matter in itself towards workability, makability, and practicality. However, he struggles with words, and thus, it is difficult to find a quote that would convey this understanding to everyone—not just software engineers. Making this clear is perhaps akin to writing a book that explains colors to a blind person. Therefore, I consider it a really big thing to realize that this precious experience happens to be the primary source of our satisfaction in the field of software design. I even heard people expressing amazement that they get paid to do this. Moreover, this sheds light on the crucial 'design decision' of making truth a person. Explaining an experience of seeing colors to a blind person is far less effective than suggesting: Try to emulate—even just a little—this singular figure from history—the Lord Jesus—and you will see colors. When even a theologian as brilliant as Ratzinger struggles to explain such fundamental concepts, it creates an opportunity for gurus to exploit. These gurus will promise far shorter and simpler books than those written by distressed, too-idealistic, and intellectually demanding popes—offering wrong answers.

Setting aside the Bible—to be discussed separately—books don't have the best track record for conveying the truth. In fact, I would argue that software may have a better one. Try reading the code of a well-designed vector graphics editor, and you will learn a great deal about the fundamental nature of two-dimensional geometry. Explore the codebase of a large investment bank, and you will gain a much deeper understanding of what money is in itself.

Now, consider a hypothetical scenario: Writing code that encapsulates the detailed experiences of numerous professional drivers.

While no one has achieved this yet, I use it here as an example because many of us drive. If you compile such hypothetical code and connect it to the steering wheel, sensors, and pedals, it will drive the car better than you could. Now, contrast this with attempting to convey the same knowledge through a thick, thousand-page book about driving. God may have created this world by thinking it, but He certainly didn't design it by delivering a long, elaborate speech.

One might argue that this is a false analogy, as software is designed to 'teach' a computer to perform specific tasks, whereas a book is intended for human readers. For example, the code required to make a car turn at precisely the correct angle in every situation is far more complex than a simple instruction in a book, such as "carefully turn the steering wheel just enough to make the car turn in the desired direction". However, in reality, a similar phrase will almost certainly appear in the code as well, serving as the name of a method or function.

If you are not interested in the details of how a particular method or function is implemented, you can continue reading the broader structure of the code. However, if you wish to delve deeper, you can examine the method where the 'careful turning' is handled in more detail. This method would define what is meant by 'just enough' or 'desired direction,' likely by referencing other pieces of code that address these concepts in even greater detail.

When writing code, you can achieve any desired level of detail, right down to instructions so elementary that even a computer can process them—such as swapping two numbers or subtracting a value from a result. Ultimately, coding is less about 'teaching' a computer and more about providing instructions with meticulous precision, presented in a way that humans can review, understand, and build upon.

Unlike books, which generally operate at a single level of abstraction, code is designed to be readable across multiple levels of detail. It often contains far more words than a book yet remains accessible to those who wish to engage with it at different layers, from high-level summaries to intricate implementations.

Most books that delve deeply into a subject are too long to read in their entirety because they must condense a complex hierarchy of abstractions into a single, linear narrative. This flattening often results in a lengthy, detailed exposition that can be difficult to navigate—especially when trying to locate specific details. Such details are typically what you seek after reading a shorter introductory book that only scratches the surface of the topic. Even if you manage to find the relevant sections, understanding them often demands significant effort to 'boot into context.' Sentences in a book are constrained by their immediate surroundings, offering little in terms of higher-level summaries or broader structural guidance.

Software, on the other hand, is free from these limitations. This superiority has been demonstrated both practically and theoretically. Practically, it is evident in the way software enables hierarchical organization, abstraction, and precise referencing, allowing users to seamlessly navigate and understand complex systems. Theoretically, it is grounded in the expressive power of programming languages. Predicate logic—the formal model for natural language—is notably less expressive than temporal logic, which serves as the foundation for standard programming languages.

The most significant difference between books and code is the level of detail they can capture while remaining comprehensible to humans. Using software, you can delve into any required level of detail. In contrast, books, articles, and other written documents often reiterate basic information again and again, with only a small portion of their content offering novel or specific insights. Nowhere is the prevalence of repetitive and redundant information more evident than in books, documents, and articles. You spend hours reading the same information over and over—a practice that may serve pedagogical purposes but stems largely from the solitary and non-collaborative nature in which books are traditionally written.

Both books and code repositories can be effectively read and understood by a trained person; it's not rocket science. Additionally, a code repository can be developed collaboratively by hundreds of people simultaneously—something that is not possible when writing a book.

It should be said that I'm definitely not against books. All forms of media that convey information have their place, and they rarely become obsolete after a new one is invented. Besides, you are currently reading a book I wrote. I just consider code repositories to be a better medium for capturing the detailed truth about how things really are (about the 'in-itselfness' of things).

Unfortunately, we don't yet have repositories for raising children, managing health issues, caring for the elderly, environmental stewardship, or Catholic doctrine. A curious person will never find answers to many detailed questions of everyday life since they are too detailed to be contained in any document, book, or article, and we have no other infrastructure available to capture them besides the heads of experienced people.

The IT managers of this world primarily view code as a means to implement functionality rather than as a way to capture the truth about things in an elegant and beautiful way—a feature often considered a welcome but secondary by-product of software development.

An extreme example of the push toward workability, makability, and practicality is the latest wave of artificial intelligence, where workability is maximized by eliminating understanding altogether.

In AI development, vast amounts of data about inputs and related outputs are used alongside logical models such as neural networks, which can be as expressive as traditional programming languages. The models are trained using enormous computational power to create configurations that generate desired outputs based on any realistic inputs. The products of this process resemble large formulas with numerous coefficients and variables, yet none of them can be described or understood in a way comprehensible to humans. This is also why—despite their ability to outperform human-written code in many applications—they tend to produce unpredictable errors (so-called hallucinations). These errors occur because the models are validated statistically rather than through a review process based on a direct understanding of the model design.

A relevant example is the repository for autonomous driving, which we discussed earlier. Currently, there is no human-written code that would capture the experience of many proficient drivers. However, it is possible to train logical models to replicate this expertise. While I am not an expert in this field, I anticipate that due to their inherent unreliability, these models will require extensive additional safety checks—code blocks to handle various contingencies—before they can be effectively deployed in production.

Since we currently lack alternatives in autonomous driving, it is better to have something rather than nothing. However, what I have just described is, without a doubt, an example of a push for *more rights* instead of doing things *more right*, a tendency characteristic of our age, just as Joseph Ratzinger described. Exploring such projects from the inside is unlikely to bring the satisfaction of witnessing something that could endure forever. The 'in-itselfness' of driving is entirely obscured for anyone reading the code.

It's difficult to imagine what it would be like if someone attempted to do something similar with their life. Perhaps it would be comparable to spending half the day in an intensive care unit just to properly enjoy life during the second half.

If there is no God and you only have a few decades left before you hit the end of your existence, this might be the most rational thing to do. However, if the opposite is true, seeking truth is almost always aimed at achieving something that could stay here forever. We will explore this further in the second part of the book, but to give you a hint, it involves the resurrection of Jesus Christ. If He has indeed risen, then it makes sense to strive to become someone who can live forever—even beyond death. In that case, aligning yourself with the truth is the right course—it can spare you from an eternity of regret over how things truly are—over the 'in-itselfness' of things.

Imagine a guy living a quiet life in a monastery, surrounded by sublime natural beauty, browsing God's repositories of truth, and spending every day in prayer. He would likely feel genuine pity for the other guy who spends half his day in intensive care so he could indulge in unlimited sex, drugs, and rock 'n' roll for the rest of it. Undoubtedly, this other guy—if he's not heartless—would genuinely pity the first guy back.

Only one of them can be right.

Randomness and Belief

When running complex software, you will always encounter various contingencies, but the behavior is never truly random. It may seem random, but there is always a sequence of steps in code execution that leads to a given situation with absolute certainty. Even when deploying a random number generator, the result only appears random unless the isolated logical universe of your software interacts with our physical world through some external device, most commonly the system clock.

For some reason, when we attempt to code a virtual world, achieving true randomness always requires mounting an 'external antenna' to the actual world. This has always puzzled me. In high school, I dreamed of writing a computer program that would function like a radio tuner with such an antenna—implemented perhaps using a Geiger-Müller counter—to decode the received noise and thereby reveal a different dimension of the universe or perhaps a different physical location in it. It was just a dream, but it reveals that the existence of randomness is really hard to swallow. First, you try to prove it's merely an illusion; when that fails, you attempt to uncover its purpose, only to fail again.

But are parts of our physical world genuinely random? Scientific exploration, particularly in quantum physics, suggests that the world does exhibit true randomness at a certain level. There is substantial evidence supporting this, although it remains a scientific theory, and as with any scientific theory, it is open to being disproved in the future, which is a fundamental aspect of the scientific method.

The logical universe in which your software runs is undoubtedly fully deterministic. The physical universe we inhabit is likely not deterministic. However, this is a belief based on evidence from meticulously conducted research rather than an established fact. Current understanding suggests that there is genuine randomness in every single atom. For some scientists, including Albert Einstein, this was difficult to accept. They envisioned the physical world as a vast, elegant software package that could be reverse-engineered from the bottom up. They hoped to discover the lower-level design patterns first, then the higher-level design decisions, and ultimately, the overall purpose of the package. In such a deterministic framework, any appearance of randomness would result merely from an incomplete understanding of the sequence of steps in code execution, leading to seemingly contingent situations.

These scientists didn't like the uncertainty of belief; they wanted to know things. They saw belief as a temporary necessity due to an imperfect understanding of how things work. They strove to get as close to the complete truth about the universe as possible, but they couldn't accept that genuine belief might be an inherent and unremovable part of it. But if genuine randomness exists in this world, then genuine belief must also exist, not just a temporary one. This has profound implications for understanding the environment in which the real world 'runs'.

Some physicists argue that the world is partially deterministic and partially random, leaving no room for free will. They contend that we cannot influence what is already predetermined, nor can we control random behavior, as doing so would imply it is not truly random. But what does it mean for something to be genuinely random?

This means that no governing rules have been discovered to explain its behavior. It could indicate that no such rules exist, or that the rules are hidden from us and yet to be uncovered, or that the source of randomness lies outside the system entirely—much like in every computer program, as discussed earlier.

Let me illustrate this with an example of an e-shop selling brushes of various sizes and purposes. Let's further imagine we are poor, shallow creatures living inside a computer system processing orders for these brushes. By analyzing the orders statistically over time, we might observe seasonality—fewer people tend to buy brushes for painting their homes during the winter. However, we might struggle to explain why certain brushes don't follow this pattern. If our thinking was confined to concepts like delivery addresses and value-added tax, we would be blind to the reality that some brushes are used for artistic purposes year-round.

Additionally, we might notice that the number of brushes sold in May can vary dramatically across different years. Without an understanding of external factors—like economic crises causing far fewer people to renovate, even during peak seasons—we might dismiss these variations as genuinely random. Within the confines of our system, this randomness would seem fundamental, even though it arises from broader realities beyond our understanding.

This analogy highlights that what appears genuinely random may not be so if we later discover aspects of the world we previously ignored. Our 'e-shop universe' might turn out to be just one part of a larger reality. Signs of this greater complexity might be found in details some of us theorize about—such as some incredibly insightful customer remarks on a few historical orders—while others dismiss them as irrelevant or nonsensical gibberish.

But is there any reason, ideally supported by experimental evidence, to believe that the genuine randomness we observe in this world originates from outside spacetime and matter?

Before World War II, Albert Einstein and Niels Bohr debated the nature of randomness. It was discovered that during certain physical processes involving particle emissions, some genuinely random properties of these particles are correlated instantaneously across vast distances. This phenomenon is known as particle entanglement.

Even when entangled particles are separated by vast distances, measuring certain random property of one particle instantly determines the corresponding property measured for the other particle. This correlation occurs faster than any physical communication could possibly travel, as it would exceed the speed of light—a violation of established physical laws.

Einstein, along with Boris Podolsky and Nathan Rosen, proposed in what became known as the EPR argument (Einstein-Podolsky-Rosen paradox) that quantum mechanics might be incomplete. They suggested that the apparent randomness of quantum mechanics could be explained by hidden local variables—properties of particles that are predetermined from the beginning but not yet measurable by us. In their view, these hidden local variables adhered to yet-undiscovered laws.

Bohr, however, countered that no such hidden variables exist, asserting that the observed behavior is genuinely random and that the correlation occurs instantaneously. In 1964, physicist John Stewart Bell devised a test to differentiate between these competing views. His work provided experimental evidence ruling out local hidden variables, demonstrating that particle properties are not predetermined by any local mechanism. Subsequent experiments have repeatedly confirmed Bell's findings. In 2022, the Nobel Prize in Physics was awarded to scientists who extended Bell's work and provided further evidence.

To conclude, in modern physics, the prevailing view holds that certain measured properties are not only genuinely random but also instantaneously synchronized, regardless of distance or time. This may suggest the existence of a phenomenon that exists outside the framework of spacetime. From a software engineer's perspective, it is as though our world operates based on a global internal state governing the randomness we observe—much like the external global source of randomness in a computer program we previously discussed (to be safe, physicists call it 'non-local').

Simply put, there appears to be something beyond spacetime—seemingly random since it's beyond our comprehension—that governs the world of matter and spacetime in a global (or 'non-local') manner. We may never find it by searching within spacetime itself; it would be akin to searching inside a virtual reality for the memory chip responsible for maintaining the internal state of the program running that virtual world.

It should be said that if something is beyond our comprehension and thus appears random, it doesn't necessarily have to be God. It could be incomprehensible because there are no rules to discover—because it simply doesn't make any sense. But why, then, is it global? Why doesn't each atom have its own local source of randomness? Why is there the instantaneous particle entanglement?

I'm not a physicist, but as a software engineer, I recognize other familiar design patterns in the structure of the world beyond the global internal state. Many of these concepts will be explored later in this book, but since this is not a book on physics, I will briefly mention a few in this chapter.

One such phenomenon in quantum physics is known as the 'superposition of states.' In this, particles genuinely appear to exist in multiple internal states simultaneously until they are measured. For example, an electron can exist in both positive and negative spin states simultaneously, but when measured, it collapses to one of these values with a certain probability. While this may seem counterintuitive in physics to many, a similar pattern is often observed in software engineering. This is known as the lazy initialization pattern.

In many cases, in your code, you work with a variable that appears to be, say, an integer (1, 2, 1234), but until you access its value, it doesn't actually exist, and any value remains possible. It's calculated just in time, when needed. The motivation behind this approach is resource efficiency. Many programs contain components that may never be used, making precomputing their values wasteful. Instead, you code everything as though the value is always there, but in fact, internally, it's only calculated when the user requests it, directly or indirectly.

Interestingly, in physics, it appears that without a conscious observer, certain values aren't 'calculated' or determined. This paradox is explored in the thought experiment known as Wigner's friend, which underscores the difficulty physicists face in reconciling the idea that the first conscious observer to examine the system plays a crucial role in determining the final value.

Physicists generally reject the notion that quantum measurement follows a 'first-come, first-served' principle, so they would likely disagree with the idea that certain physical variables are initialized in a lazy manner. In such a view, the 'served' entities would be conscious observers, and most physicists oppose incorporating a 'conscious observer topology' into all experimental models, as that would *scandalously* recognize consciousness as an inherent dimension of reality.

Einstein famously asked: "Do you really believe the moon is not there when you are not looking at it?" One might be tempted to question how a man who based his famous theories on the principle that distance cannot be measured without a physical meter and time cannot be measured without a physical clock could, de facto, ask: Why can't we measure without someone *willing* to facilitate the measurement?

If the world were like a vast, elegant software system and God were the source of all randomness within it, it might seem as though He waits for a conscious observer before assigning values to certain variables in His internal state. One might ask, why would He wait—if not to allow for the existence of genuine free will in conscious observers?

Physicists also grapple with explaining the apparent continuity and infinite divisibility of classical physics compared to the quantized, discrete states observed in quantum physics.

But isn't this precisely how we would implement a virtual reality—by calculating each new snapshot of time using discrete sets of options (operators) and retrospectively maintaining the appearance of a seamless spacetime continuum that aligns with geometrical principles?

Doesn't it feel natural that when observing stars—where we see only the past—everything appears predetermined, like a seamless movie? Yet, when examining how the edge of the future is being constructed, we observe a discrete set of possible futures from which conscious observers are allowed to choose. Isn't this the intuitive personal experience of every one of us?

Unfortunately, even if physicists devise an experiment demonstrating that time is quantized per conscious observer and that a minimum measurable time interval exists, it would still fall short of proving that God is who He is.

After all, even if God lived among us, performed miracles daily, and spoke words of eternal life, many would still reject Him. We have historical and experimental evidence for this, as we will explore later in this book.

Continuing the analogy of a vast and elegant software package, it should be said many prominent scientists believed that someone indeed designed this package, and for many of them, that designer was God.

We know this because many were Catholic priests, including physicist Father Georges Lemaître, the author of the Big Bang theory, who dared to challenge the prevailing anti-biblical scientific consensus of the nineteen fifties—which still held that the universe had no origin—only to be mocked for his 'big bang theories' by renowned astronomer Fred Hoyle during a BBC radio broadcast.

I argue that without allowing inherent randomness in His 'software package', God would eliminate a straightforward infrastructure for intervening in everyday matters. The code of the package would forever be given 'as created,' and based on the initial values of the variables that make up the initial internal state, the sequence of future states of the world could be deterministically calculated. This means that the only way for God to intervene after the Big Bang would be to change some values of the variables during the package's execution. This is akin to using a debugger during software execution—pausing the program, manually changing values, and then resuming execution. Such interventions could be considered miracles. This is how you multiply loaves of bread. However, too many miracles could make the laws of physics appear inconsistent or impossible to infer, as some significant miracles might leave traces that would falsify scientific theories about how the world works. In other words, such a design decision by God could make the world appear as a difficult-to-understand, inconsistent mess.

With almost complete certainty, we don't observe miraculous inconsistencies that violate established scientific theories anywhere around. Furthermore, in a deterministic world, human free will would be an illusion. If God had already programmed the entire story of the universe before its execution began, why would He even want to get involved?

The inherent randomness of nature addresses all these design concerns: The truth about how the world works can still be discovered, albeit in stochastic terms. Every possible experimental outcome can be predicted with a certain probability, allowing for the possibility of frequent God's interventions without undermining scientific theories. From this perspective, not all of God's actions qualify as miracles.

Moreover, inherent genuine randomness allows for the existence of free will without making the world unintelligible. Thus, genuine randomness provides a compelling reason to view ourselves as active agents rather than mere biological machines. It also allows the world to remain intelligible and comprehensible while still permitting God to act extensively as a 'living God' who is actively present rather than a distant deity who was only involved at the beginning and now merely observes from afar. This perspective aligns with the idea that seeking truth and getting closer to the rule of truth (or, in Catholic terms, to the Kingdom of God) opens the streambed through which love can flow from God to us to nurture children of this world—His children. We will shed more light on all of this in the final chapter of the first part of this book.

Of course, you don't have to believe any of this. Belief is always a decision, a choice in your private realm. However, the evidence on which you make that decision is not subjective at all. There remains a probability that all of this—however strange it may seem—is mere randomness, a series of coincidences devoid of purpose or meaning.

In a world designed like ours, we will never know for sure: If there is genuine randomness, there must also be genuine belief.

— 9 —

Before Christ

In the previous chapters, I argued that pursuing truth should be our highest priority in life. I also demonstrated that in a world like ours, the existence of genuine randomness could allow for profound divine intervention in all matters. In software terms, the framework of this world appears to have an interface that could potentially enable the workings of Providence.

In our lives, events can either be purely accidental, partially random, having no deeper sense, or they can imbued with significance and meaning. One of these options must be true, but no matter how hard you try to find patterns or attribute things to pure coincidence, you can never attain certainty—this is by design. It is a deeply personal choice based on the evidence you collect in your private realm (not in any books of wisdom). Your decision—right or wrong—will carry immense practical implications in your life.

Even if you pray, "Dear Lord, if you really exist, please give me a sign that will be clearly recognizable and understandable to me, even if it's absolutely incommunicable to anyone else," and you receive such a sign—and you likely will—you might still interpret it as a meaningless coincidence rather than evidence of anything divine. This is why the positions of believers and nonbelievers are so close.

If you value the truth above everything else, there is no other way than to wrestle with this question seriously, even if a final resolution remains elusive.

Some people argue that they refuse to live as though God exists until they see compelling evidence of His existence. To me, however, it seems more reasonable to live as if God exists until evidence suggests otherwise. If life truly has no inherent meaning and the only rational goal is to maximize pleasure before death, I wouldn't mind choosing instead a life filled with purpose and meaning. After all, if death is merely the 'off switch' of a biological machine, I would never realize my mistake.

Call me a 'useful idiot' if you like—I won't mind. The ability to enjoy life depends on living in a society built by our 'unenjoying' ancestors, who toiled selflessly to create a world that functions, at least to some extent. Without their efforts, we would simply suffer until our deaths, experiencing only very limited pleasures. I consider it an honor to join their ranks—even if you choose to call it the 'Useful Idiots Club.'

Moreover, as I've tried to demonstrate, in a functioning society trying to enjoy your life as much as you can before you die may be—in reality—the surest path to suffering until your death. Of course, I may be biased by my own observations. But don't take my word for it—see for yourself, as part of your first-hand baby-like private research.

Our ancestors didn't live in a society that worked as well as ours. They didn't have things under control to the extent they could start thinking about getting everything under control: Hoping to eliminate contingency, aspiring to bring more and more evidence on the altar of nature's determinism that would ultimately show any God would have no actual means to substantially interfere over the absolute rule of matter that exists with no intellect behind it.

That is, with no intellect behind, except for an educated, progressive man, who is, at the same time, no more than an imperfect biological machine predestined to crave pleasure, explicitly or implicitly.

This is how Ratzinger describes this relatively new religious belief that now seems as if it were lifted from the pages of Jules Verne:

The most consequential form of atheism, Marxism, asserts the unity of all being in its strictest form by declaring that all being is matter. In doing so, being itself is entirely separated from the earlier concept of the Absolute, which is linked to the idea of God. However, it simultaneously acquires features that make its absoluteness clear, thus reminding us once again of the idea of God.

(...)

Monotheism assumes that the Absolute is consciousness, which knows humanity and can communicate with it; for materialism, the Absolute—as Matter—is stripped of all personal attributes and can in no way be related to the concepts of call and answer.

With the environmental crisis looming due to our naive and reckless manipulation of nature, and given the current state of scientific understanding, we find ourselves in a situation increasingly reminiscent of that faced by our ancestors.

Moreover, to a hypothetical software designer crafting a virtual universe on a laptop, even the nature of matter might seem secondary to his design, or at least not the necessary backbone that holds everything together. Why would anyone design a world that would be solely about matter? It would be like creating software with no purpose, merely to adhere to a specific methodology or naming convention, with no motivation, no requirements, and no user story behind it.

Today, we can no longer be Marxists, given the experience and evidence we've accumulated, unless we have exchanged the pursuit of truth for self-esteem.

Still, to many, Marxists may appear to simply propose replacing a 'nonexistent God' with an innocuous 'reasonable agreement' among 'all people,' aiming to create a society of comfort and peace on earth. This perspective partially makes sense because, in this view, there isn't just one educated, progressive individual exerting control over the 'absolute matter' (world's resources)—there are many. However, some of these individuals may pursue pleasure far more effectively than others, potentially becoming oppressors who, in Marxist terms, limit the human rights of the less fortunate—the oppressed.

If God—as the ultimate source of all unconditional love and care received indirectly through society—is dismissed as an illusion, the logical outcome is a dynamic of conflict—what Marxists call class warfare.

At first glance, the idea of policing such dynamics at the state level through a 'legal agreement' may seem appealing. It can easily be branded as a Christian-like struggle for the poor, sick, and marginalized, which partly explains why billions of people around the world have supported Marxism in various forms.

While this may be seen as uplifting evidence that people naturally gravitate toward Christianity, it is crucial to explore why such 'legal agreements' cannot replace God's love. Instead, they inevitably degenerate into totalitarian systems marked by state brutality and individual mercilessness.

Imagine a group of individuals who legitimately require special accommodations: For instance, Christian pacifists who, on the grounds of faith, refuse to bear arms or participate in war under any circumstance. Fair enough! Let's grant them the right to conscientious objection. We always fight for more rights for the people! After all, it's conceivable that some Christians feel divinely called to strict pacifism, just as others may feel called to military service. Who would object?

However, what happens when others begin exploiting this exception? Suppose a group of people starts falsely claiming pacifist beliefs simply to avoid the inconvenience of military service. Clearly, this would pose a threat to the integrity of the 'reasonable agreement,' and measures would be needed to address it. Enter a 'reasonable' solution: Requiring every claimant to pass a lie detector test before being granted an exemption. No problem!

But this actually introduces new problems. Genuine Christian pacifists, now all viewed as potential fraudsters, must prove the sincerity of their convictions. Many would likely become nervous during the lie detector test and fail—not due to dishonesty, but because of the intimidating circumstances. The process fosters mistrust and subjects sincere individuals to humiliation and unfair scrutiny.

But surely our enlightened state officials—whom we all so greatly admire for their wisdom—will empathize with them and bend the rules a bit when it's reasonable! The wise comrade commissar tasked with adjudicating exemptions might turn a blind eye and dismiss these 'edge cases' as harmless anomalies! That is, unless, of course, they hold personal biases against Christians. In that case, they could exploit their authority to target, oppress, and become corrupt. What began as a 'reasonable agreement' devolves into suspicion, bureaucracy, corruption, and, ultimately, omnipresent abuse of power.

We have considered just one small issue—military service. Now, imagine applying this approach to every aspect of society. The result is inevitable: A descent into state fascism, where the state controls everything, replaces God, and elevates the comrade commissars into a ruthless ruling elite. Society fractures into two fundamental groups: Marxist believers and nonbelievers.

For nonbelievers, social standing depends entirely on connections: Who they can ask for favors among the enlightened commissars and how high those connections reach. Meanwhile, Marxist believers see themselves as imbued with a divine purpose, fueling their relentless climb up the ladder of power. Their trajectory, however, often oscillates—rising to positions of influence, descending into political prisons, and rising again—determined by their mercilessness, strength, and sheer luck in navigating the system's brutal dynamics.

Some might argue, "Doesn't every society governed by laws face this risk?" The answer is: It certainly does not. Societies that do not attempt to replace God with bureaucratic paperwork of a 'reasonable agreement' view laws and regulations as a necessary evil rather than embracing them as a utopian roadmap to paradise.

This distinction matters. In such societies, officials are compelled to prioritize the will of the voters, striving to keep the electorate satisfied in order to retain their positions in the next election cycle. Nobody sees them as enlightened, wise guardians of traditional values who can bend the rules at will. They are not deemed divine, nor do they see themselves that way. This dynamic serves as a check against autocracy. In contrast, when the state is seen as the ultimate authority, officials become untouchable autocrats. They are no longer accountable to the very people they are meant to serve and protect from oppression.

Obviously, the ultimate oppressor is never the state itself but rather the belief that enlightened individuals are the only cunning intellects ruling over the 'absolute matter.' Without this belief, class warfare would not be regarded as a natural law, nor would the idea of a state mafia 'protecting us from itself' seem a primordial force within the laws of the universe.

When I was a kid living in Central Europe, in a region recently vacated by Russian occupation troops, I remember being puzzled by a number of haughty individuals who behaved as if they were of almost divine origin. They had no higher social status, wealth, education, or intelligence—some were even poor manual workers. Yet, they exuded a merciless sense of superiority that I couldn't understand. I felt deep disdain for them back then, during my elementary school years—a sentiment that left a lasting mark on my perception of my own nation, one I am still trying to fully recover from.

These people have since disappeared altogether, and I now believe that what I witnessed back then were true Marxist believers—people convinced they were the only intellects behind the matter. Having done some recent private research in that area, I found that even now, 30 years later, many of these individuals still exist in their original form in the former Soviet (Marxist) bloc, exhibiting the same ruthlessness and baseless sense of superiority.

Interestingly, they sometimes adopt Christian symbols and rites much like the Romans used their polytheistic 'religio' to express loyalty to their empire—adorned with the grand aesthetics of religious observance without a necessary faith in the supernatural. Their god has been effectively tamed; they can label it a 'Christian god,' but only if it remains powerless in the Marxist sense—stripped of any means of influence with no interface to interfere—an empty custom. Some even go so far as to refer to themselves as the 'Third Rome.'

It now makes sense to me that no one can feel more on top of creation than a believing Marxist. Obviously, this kind of existence is unsustainable in any society that values meritocracy to any extent; only in a totalitarian regime can it survive.

In a sense, Marx takes us back to a time before Christ, reviving the specter of a primordial force in the universe to which we must constantly pay ransom for protection against that very force—a concept once embodied by Moloch or Baal. If behind all matter there is only random noise and the only intellect is ours, we are as doomed as our ancestors who once sacrificed their newborns slaving to those deities. Marxism inevitably leads to a bloody clash among all believing Marxists, as only one of them can claim the position of supreme intellect over all creation.

In the Russian empire (formerly Soviet), this ordering is currently referred to as 'the vertical of power,' where a hierarchy of subservient individuals and their aspiring slave masters is headed by a brutal overlord in the flesh. In such a society, all human relationships degenerate into dynamics of stronger versus weaker, masters versus slaves.

The same Marxist dynamics—often manipulatively advertised as either a pro-Christian or anti-Christian fight for the poor, sick, and marginalized—can currently be observed in many countries around the world, not just in the former Soviet bloc.

But let's return to the design concerns now. If God designed this world, then understanding His motivation, at least to some extent, is essential to forming a true image of Him. Our ancestors couldn't ask a question that we've only recently been able to consider: How would I design a world, and why? They felt far more at the mercy of nature's forces. Despite their best efforts to do things right, they still faced significant unpredictability. With intellects similar to ours, they concluded that if their lives were to be more than temporary, senseless suffering ending in death, there must be some deeper meaning behind everything happening to them. They made a choice strikingly similar to the one I outlined at the beginning of this chapter: They chose purpose and meaning over nihilism and death—they decided to found a 'Useful Idiots Club,' as the enlightened Lenins of this world say, condescending from their divine point of view. And since meaning always requires an intellect to bestow it, they reasoned that the world was likely designed as a 'multi-player' environment, with this intellect—God—being the most significant player. They found it reasonable to communicate with Him, so they prayed—for prayer is a natural and essential act for anyone who seeks meaning in life (many of us pray unwittingly).

Humanity's lived experience—not just some philosophical theory—is crucial in building a true image of God. Before Christ, pagan people not only lacked the experience of designing through pure thought (such as coding), but they also had no understanding of how God would behave if He were to incarnate as a man. This lack of experience led them to create the original image of God as an immensely mighty and cruel invisible monarch—one they believed required appeasement through sacrifice. From today's Christian perspective, this might seem like the gravest debt to truth one could ever incur—the gravest sin of willingly submitting to evil. However, at the time, the only powerful rulers in flesh people knew were tyrannical overlords who enslaved those around them.

Imagine living under the notion that no matter how virtuous you are, you are at the mercy of a malevolent invisible ruler who demands extortion in the form of sacrifice. These people often sacrificed their firstborn children, clinging to the false hope that this would make their lives more bearable.

Imagine their anguish—their deep, desperate longing for a savior.

Ratzinger writes:

> In the history of religion, the God-Son is said to have pre-
> ceded the God-Father. More accurately, one should say that
> God the Savior, the Redeemer, appears before God the Cre-
> ator.

Even a devout atheist must, on some level, recognize how the coming of Christ ultimately saved these poor pagans from their sins and from Satan's power. Today, no one worships Moloch or Baal.

Christ revealed the true image of God as the source of all uncondi-
tional love in the world—a vision that gave rise to cultures that cancel Baal, Moloch, and Marx.

— 10 —

Word

If matter does not play the central role in the world's design, if *light is not photons* and *the world is not atoms*, we might dare to ask whether there is something more real, more fundamental than atoms and photons—a building block without which this world, as we know it, could not exist. Atoms and photons are models of behavior that allow us to predict reactions to our actions, but they are merely elegant descriptions in our minds, not the actual *stuff* that responds with reactions to our actions. So, is there something more palpable than that?

If the world were truly an elegant software package—which it is not!—the key to understanding it would be its source code. In programming, the fundamental unit of source code is the 'word' (though it may have different names in computer science).

During the execution of a software package, it is also common to receive reactions in response to our actions, typically referred to as input and output. Also in this case, the actual *stuff* that responds is almost always intangible. However, an experienced engineer can envision the design that produces the specific behavior and, with enough data, can even write code in a programming language of choice to replicate the same behavior—an output for an input, a reaction for an action. If the original author was a good programmer and the investigating engineer as well, very likely their codes would be semantically identical, sometimes even almost wholly identical—if they understood the thing in itself in the same way.

Behaviors modeled by software are not necessarily physical processes; in fact, they rarely are. However, when physical world simulations are created, it is unlikely that photons and atoms are used very often, as that would be too cumbersome in most cases. What is certain is that if we possess the source code, we do not need to theorize about the underlying concepts behind the observed behavior; we can simply read the code to see what's really there.

So, are there photons and atoms in God's mind, assuming He created this world? My hunch is that there are, though it is merely an unfounded feeling, driven by my admiration for the elegance of photons and atoms.

However, at times, it almost seems to me as though photons have overshadowed everything else. I feel a profound sadness that we leave so many other aspects of His design unexplored, unmapped, and undescribed in an equally elegant manner—primarily using software, not books, to achieve the extreme level of detail. Among other things, this would make shallow lies (sins) much easier to discern, and it would also make general artificial intelligence possible.

Allow me to quote perhaps the most well-known passage of the Bible. I believe it merits a fresh reading in this context:

> [1] In the beginning was the Word
>   and the Word was with God
>   and the Word was God.
> [2] The Word was with God in the beginning.
> [3] Everything came into being through the Word,
>   and without the Word nothing came into being.
> [4] What came into being through the Word was life,
>   and the life was the light for all people.
> [5] The light shines in the darkness,
>   and the darkness doesn't extinguish the light.
>
> **John 1:1–5 (CEB)**

Regardless of how God designed the world or what is in His mind, the word plays an absolutely key role in this world—far beyond all software analogies.

Firstly, words are not merely pointers to worldly things; they exist on their own and, in that sense, may be the most tangible part of existence we can encounter.

Secondly, words are the only means by which we can receive testimony from others—our neighbors—allowing us to understand what's in their hearts, imagine ourselves in their shoes, and understand the world with their eyes. And that makes God's presence much less uncertain than so far discussed. Let me explain.

Scientific exploration or philosophy can be pursued as a solitary enterprise. While practically difficult, it is theoretically possible. You can create a theory alone and run a series of experiments in various settings to ensure it cannot be easily refuted. You can do it independently, without any assistance, provided that you are able to conduct enough experiments to achieve a sufficient level of certainty in your findings.

In philosophy, it's similar. Up to this point, we have mostly engaged in philosophy, as I have deliberately minimized the use of the Word. Even when contemplating God, you can formulate philosophical theories. However, since a substantial part of your thinking will involve your private realm and your inner life, you will only have one test subject: Yourself. And that is never enough. You can rigorously examine your ideas and discipline yourself the best you can to avoid subjective bias. However, if you are not to become a fanatic and your conclusions are meant to be more than formal logical inferences, you will never attain the same level of certainty when contemplating God alone as you would be able to achieve by conducting proper scientific research in solitude.

To truly immerse yourself in a faith solid enough to bring you inner peace, you need other people. You must live in a community to share with others your deepest thoughts, fears, doubts, and experiences with prayer, things transcendent, and God. As you discover that your inner experiences are similar or even identical to your neighbors, you will achieve—step by step—a level of certainty in your faith truly comparable to that obtained from repeated experiments in different settings in the field of science.

Of course, this does not eliminate the risk of shared illusions—just as the scientific method does not fully guard against false paradigms, as history has repeatedly shown.

Just as a single experiment in science can offer a hint but is far from enough to establish someone as a scientist, so too is one person's individual experience insufficient to qualify them as faithful, let alone as a theologian. This may be hard for individualist intellectuals to accept, especially those who believe they can theorize in isolation, drawing solely on the works of other like-minded thinkers. They may celebrate their creative freedom and imagine they contribute new, original perspectives, applying *rigid* or *flexible* logic to the ideas of their predecessors. However, such efforts often result in the creation of systematic nonsense. Ratzinger engages with some of the most enlightened recent names in his book, but I lack both the space and the expertise to do the same here.

As a contrast to the individualist intellectual, I would elevate the village priest. Village priests typically don't write theology, nor are they usually allowed to do so. They don't engage in creative, free-thinking exercises to produce new wisdom, and they may not always be eloquent speakers or intellectual giants. Yet, they serve as the vital heart of their community's lived experience with God at a given time and place. If there is anyone who possesses the most *experimental data* about faith in a given time and place, it is the village priest. They gather and accumulate this experience to guide people through their private baby-like research in their private realms since this is where the real struggle for God happens, not in any books of wisdom.

You can buy a fridge that someone else has invented, designed, and manufactured, but you cannot buy a faith that someone else invented, designed, and manufactured. Faith is your own research, your own endeavor, and your own relationship with God, which can only be accomplished within a community of people intimately sharing their lives. If you seek to deepen your faith, look to a humble, ordinary village priest rather than a wise, free-thinking, eloquent guru.

Ratzinger writes:

> Man comes into contact with God by coming into contact with fellow human beings. Faith is essentially oriented towards the You and the We; only through this dual connection does it unite man with God. This means, conversely, that the relationship with God and the relationship with one's fellow human beings are inseparable in the inner structure of faith. The relationship to God, to the You, and to the We interweave and do not stand side by side.

> From another perspective, we could express the same idea by saying that God wants to approach men only through men; He seeks the human being only in their fellow humanity.

> (...)

> God does not appear in logistical calculations. Perhaps our

difficulty in speaking about God today arises from the fact that our language increasingly tends to become pure calculation—it is becoming more and more a mere code of technical communication and less and less a means of contact within the Logos of our shared being, in which the Foundation of all things is also touched, either intuitively or consciously.

And he even includes an anecdote that fits well here from the life of another consequential saint—Augustine of Hippo:

Augustine recounts in his Confessiones how a pivotal moment in his own journey was learning that the renowned philosopher Marius Victorinus had become a Christian. Victorinus had long refused to join the Church, believing that his philosophy already encompassed everything essential to Christianity and that he was in full agreement with its fundamental spiritual principles. Since he could already claim the central Christian ideas as his own through philosophical thinking, he saw no need for his convictions to be institutionalized through Church membership.

To summarize, faith only truly works when practiced in a community, among friends as close as your family. You cannot achieve a firmly rooted faith by listening to a charismatic religious leader—a guru. Gurus are opaque because they are roles rather than persons. They are not your family or your peers; it is extremely dangerous to get intimate with them. They may even provide accurate insights but can never give you the level of certainty in transcendent matters that comes from a lived community of peers, equals, neighbors, and friends who have shared their lives, including their inner lives, for years. You cannot delegate your faith—it will always remain your private endeavor. The responsibility to seek the truth is only yours and cannot be outsourced to any guru, superior, or institution.

In matters concerning God and in all non-material matters in general, you need fellow neighbors to achieve a similar level of certainty you achieve via scientific research in the world of physical phenomena. I can honestly say that in our parish, in our community, we all experience the same God in very similar ways. However, we will never be able to produce experimental data sheets upon request proving this; you would have to become one of us.

In my time, many would be tempted to say—however weird it may sound—that this is the most pivotal evidence ruling out God's significant presence in everyday matters. I hope it can be seen more clearly now why this is total nonsense.

A solid faith in God is only achievable within a community. In Catholic terms, this community is referred to as the Church (or a local church). I'm not speaking of the Church as an institution here.

The Church has a collective memory that includes Sacred Scripture (the Bible). Also, it encompasses the Magisterium and Sacred Tradition—teachings that, while not part of the Bible, are rooted in it or have been passed down since the time of the apostles.

The Bible—often called the word of God—is a collection of texts that have been critically selected and meticulously maintained by the Church—a community of close people, often likened to a family, that has shared its experiences with God continuously for thousands of years as a living body, an organism. Only those texts deemed 'divinely inspired' made it into the final collection, while many others were excluded from the Bible.

The Bible can be considered divinely inspired to the extent that it helps the community find a truthful relationship with God. It is a collection of testimonies chronicling humanity's encounters with God across millennia.

Reading the Bible outside the context of the Church may lead to misunderstandings and misinterpretations, much like trying to grasp the intricacies of a company by reading its meeting notes without having any insider experience.

— 11 —

Word in Practice

When I was young, my father taught me that all human beings are inherently selfish. He believed that what appears to be altruism is merely an illusion because even when we act for the good of others, we are ultimately driven by our own satisfaction. According to him, no matter how selfless a deed may seem, it is always rooted in the pursuit of our own inner pleasure—a truth that, upon closer examination, becomes evident.

I was not born into a Christian family, so I initially adopted the same beliefs as my parents. However, as I began to closely examine my own experiences, I gradually realized that this notion of inherent selfishness wasn't true. My father never suggested that doing good was wrong—such an idea would defy logic—and I saw him do good things. So naturally, I focused on doing what I believed to be good without worrying too much about whether these actions were properly selfish or not.

What I found very soon was that doing what I felt was right demonstrably didn't bring me any sense of pleasure, which I had regarded then as the opposite of suffering. I lived in a freshly post-communist society where my classmates and teachers often reacted with hostility when I—for instance—called things by their true names. I was baptized, but my parents were neither Christians nor communists, and they didn't equip me with enough knowledge of the accepted patterns of behavior in our society. I didn't know the particulars of the Original Sin at that time and place. Many people, including my teachers, warned my parents that my life would end poorly if I continued with my attitude. And I agreed—it seemed like the most likely outcome.

I began to question why I was drawn to actions that alienated me from society when I was supposed to live a life of selfish pleasure. Over time, I realized that there was something within me—a kind of inner voice—that compelled me to do what was right. I concluded that I followed this voice because, in some way, I loved what it stood for, though it is difficult to put into words. Though I suffered, I did so with love.

Looking back, I now recognize that what I experienced was a manifestation of what the Catholic faith refers to as the Holy Spirit. I've come to realize that this experience is common within our parish community, making it feel quite natural to me now.

As a child, I sought an alternative explanation for how society functioned, and this led me to discover the Gospels. When I read them, I was struck by how deeply I was able to identify with Jesus' worldview and, to some extent, with his life story. He was the first person I truly connected with, becoming my real role model. Today, I understand that this experience is also nothing unusual—it's something all Christians share.

St. Paul summarizes this experience when he says:

> 3 Therefore I want you to know that no one speaking
>   by the [power and influence of the] Spirit of God
>   can say, "Jesus be cursed," and no one
>   can say, "Jesus is [my] Lord," except
>   by [the power and influence of] the Holy Spirit.
>   **1 Corinthians 12:3 (AMP)**

The divinely inspired word of the Bible—first of all, the Gospels—often feels as if you read the source code and suddenly see *what's really there.* If you have accurately thought about a certain subject based on your first-hand experience, it usually gives you validation while also providing the proper context and revealing implications you might not have considered. The word is always ahead of you. What you read is often so astonishing that it makes you doubt it could have come from a man without divine inspiration—let alone someone who lived thousands of years ago. Suddenly, you're struck with awe: Could it be that God truly exists?

Ratzinger writes:

> In other words, faith gives precedence to the word over thought, which structurally distinguishes it from the nature of philosophy. In philosophy, thought precedes the word, for philosophy is the product of reflection—something one then

seeks to express in words, which, however, always remain secondary to thought and are therefore fundamentally replaceable by other words.

Faith, by contrast, approaches man from the outside, and this external origin is essential to it. Faith is—to repeat it once more—not something self-conceived but something spoken to me, something that confronts me as neither self-invented nor conceivable, something that calls me and places me under obligation.

On the other hand, since the word reaches us in a form that was once written and thus fixed permanently, there are times when its meaning may elude us—even within the context of the Church and despite the guidance of learned scholars. The full meaning—and its depth—gradually reveals itself over time as humanity undergoes diverse experiences. These experiences, alongside the word, shape our evolving understanding of the true image of God.

Clearly, this process isn't always a straightforward one. I've always been fascinated by how the Church, as an institution, could provide answers to so many questions. Yet, there were times when I completely disagreed with certain answers, finding the official explanations insufficient or even questionable. However, as I delved deeper into these subjects, I invariably discovered that the answers were correct, even when the explanations were indeed lacking or flawed (sometimes also the questions).

I often wondered what kind of institution this was—one that consistently had the right answers but struggled to derive them properly? My current understanding is that some answers were once more apparent to a broader audience, but over time, their quality explanations were lost or became ineffective. This, in part, likely reflects the challenge of human intellect attempting to interpret knowledge that originates from the infinitely superior intellect of God.

The following chapter may give an example of this.

— 12 —

Name of God

In the Catholic Creed—the central prayer that encapsulates the core beliefs of the faith—it is proclaimed that God "has spoken through the prophets." While these words of God, preserved in the Bible, may not always be verifiable through historical and archeological evidence, they have endured through the faith of countless generations within the Church, who have found them to be inspired by God again and again through their personal search for truth, similar to the *private baby-like research* discussed earlier.

Though their societies may have been far less technologically advanced than ours, these individuals were often far more proficient at eliminating self-deceptions and pursuing the truth on the personal level in their specific life circumstances. In this regard, one could argue that we have become underdeveloped because many of us have not been properly catechized. The phrases we now have to take 'as they are' were once expressions in the contemporary language of their time, readily understood by all. I pray I could contribute, at least a bit, to changing this in the second half of this book.

We cannot simply dismiss the intellectual achievements of those who lived before us because they didn't have refrigerators in their kitchens. After all, most of us simply purchase refrigerators—a task far less intellectually demanding than designing and constructing them. Truth, however, cannot be bought in the same way as refrigerators. The pursuit of truth is a personal endeavor that cannot be delegated to anyone else without compromising one's humanity. Our ancestors—whether kings or peasants—were capable of undertaking this demanding intellectual work. They have my respect. Dismissing them as primitives would be deeply condescending. Seeking purpose and meaning in life should be a natural priority for everyone—far more essential than buying the products of those who have mastered the laws of physics.

We have the word of God and the word of man—two crucial sources in our pursuit of truth. Both must be approached critically, as even God's word reaches us through the mouth of man. Reading the Bible, in essence, is reading parchment texts penned by our ancestors thousands of years ago, capturing their experience with God and their own personal quest for truth. Some passages recount historical events, others take the form of poetry or song; some are meant to be interpreted metaphorically, others literally—and at times, we are unsure. While certain parts may currently seem incomprehensible to many, none of them can be considered irrelevant. If they were, they simply wouldn't be included. Some texts were even excluded from the Bible because they were not deemed essential.

Today, expressing what's in your heart can sometimes be more effective through a song or rap verses; other times, through a blog post or a book. In this way, the word of God and the word of man are alike—they both take different forms to reach deeper.

But does it also work the other way around? Can we peer into God's heart and empathize with Him based on His word? Certainly, through the words of man, we can empathize with those closest to us—our friends, family, and neighbors. To truly know someone is to understand them from the inside, to feel their internal struggles, and perhaps to glimpse the unique purpose God has given them. But can we, through the word of God—alongside prayer, our inner voice, and the insights from the lives of others—come to know God from within?

Let's embark on a thought experiment to explore how the word of God might gradually reveal itself.

Imagine you exist in a void—nothing else is present. There is no Earth, no stars, no laws of physics, and no personal history of yours. It's just you and your creative potential—like a software engineer able to design by thought alone, without the need for a cumbersome laptop. How does it feel? How would you start? Take a few minutes to reflect on this. We'll delve into these questions later. But first, consider this:

What is your name?

You could choose any arbitrary name, but that wouldn't truly define you. It would, therefore, make no sense. You might consider calling yourself 'Love' since, as Christian street evangelists often sing, *God is love*. But there are too few things to love yet—you haven't created the universe. Love could only be fully realized after you allow creation to unfold and evolve, culminating in human beings capable of understanding love. But even if you tried explaining that you were 'Love' to an early human, they likely wouldn't grasp it. It's a complex idea that requires a foundation, otherwise it's just a sound. You would need an entire nation and several millennia to convey it through practical, lived experience.

As you further reflect on this, you may find that your situation somewhat mirrors Descartes' famous statement, "Cogito, ergo sum"—"I think, therefore I am." Descartes sought an indubitable truth and found that if one can think, explore, and question ('cogitare'), then at least their existence is undeniable. In your case, however, you don't question your own existence—it is the foundation of all that you are. In fact, existence and you are currently one and the same.

As Ratzinger writes:

> (...) Being is believed to be a person, and the person is believed to be Being itself (...).

You are a blank slate, unburdened by inherited limitations like the Original Sin. Isn't this the unspoken assumption that Ratzinger criticized in Descartes' method? So perhaps the phrase isn't so flawed after all; it just needs to be reversed in your case: "I am, therefore I think." But even that falls short, as you are not compelled to think or create—you do so willingly. Thus, "I am, and I intend to design by thought" seems more fitting. However, since you intend not only to design but also to deeply engage with the world after its creation, even that phrase feels too restrictive. The simplest, most profound expression of your essence is simply: "I am." That would be your name.

Now, let's examine one of the Bible's most profound passages. God appears to Moses in the form of a burning bush and gives him the mission to lead the Israelites out of Egypt. Moses, filled with fear, wonders—as Ratzinger notes—how a people accustomed to polytheism would respond. They might ask which of the many gods Moses had encountered. Thus, Moses asks God for His name.

¹³ Then Moses said to God,
    "If I come to the people of Israel and say to them,
    'The God of your fathers has sent me to you,'
    and they ask me, 'What is his name?'
    what shall I say to them?"
    God said to Moses,
¹⁴   "I am who I am." And he said,
    "Say this to the people of Israel,
    'I am has sent me to you.'"   **Ex 3:13–14 (ESV)**

There has been considerable debate among scholars about the best translation of the phrase often rendered as "I am who I am." The original Hebrew, Ehyeh Asher Ehyeh, is more literally translated as "I am that I am." Some scholars interpret it as "I am he that is," "I exist because I exist," "I remain who I have always been," or "I will be who I will be," among various other interpretations. Some scholars suggest that God's response to Moses conveys a touch of frustration, almost as if He refuses to answer directly. Others, however, interpret the phrase as a profound affirmation of God's presence, suggesting that it conveys the message that God is the one who is always there for His people.

However, as Ratzinger points out, God's name is reiterated when He says, "I am has sent me to you." Therefore, in line with our software analogy, the first phrase could as well be understood as a simple yet profound declaration: "I am I am."

Through this thought experiment, I sought to demonstrate two key points.

First, I wanted to illustrate how the word of God can gradually unveil as human experience and understanding evolve, emphasizing how shortsighted it would be to dismiss the Bible merely because some parts may be difficult to grasp at certain points in history.

Second, I wanted to express my ongoing fascination with how, after engaging in some speculative reflection—if we get things right—we can suddenly uncover a passage in the Bible that feels so ahead of its time it almost seems as though the Bible itself has been *hacked*—if not for the fact that the printed version on my table remains unchanged.

13

Anthropomorphic God

So far, I have described God in a seemingly anthropomorphic way—as if He were a person. Not a person of flesh and blood, but still an intellect with a deep understanding of humanity, capable of communication. I mentioned such communication occurs through our inner voice via the Holy Spirit, but also through actual words in the case of the prophets and even other individuals. While rare, such experiences are not so uncommon that one might never meet someone who has had them. However, it's far from certain that God truly possesses anthropomorphic qualities. This question warrants deeper exploration.

I. In ancient times, people believed in many gods. These deities were often local, tied to places where people encountered profound spiritual experiences: A god of a miraculous well, a god of a magnificent old tree, and so on. Christianity swept these gods off the face of the earth as fairy tales—in the literal sense. It should be said it doesn't mean Catholics somehow ceased to have spiritual experiences when confronted with breathtaking natural scenery. Personally, I feel incredibly honored and gifted to live on this planet almost every time I venture into the countryside near my home. That said, I don't believe in fairytales because the related phenomena aren't scientifically detectable. I have also never encountered anything of that nature myself, not even in my inner life, nor have any of the people I am close to—whether in my parish community or among those I trust—reported such experiences. In my experience, polytheism is not real.

II. I also don't have much to say about Moloch and Baal, the evil intellects worshipped before the coming of Christ (though comparatively less among Jews). These deities were revered in hopes of securing prosperity, fertility, or victory in battle, ultimately enslaving those who sought their favor. Today, there is no one left to worship them, at least not in an overtly religious way. No one offers their newborns as sacrifices to these gods, and the world, in many ways, is arguably in better shape than it was then. We have not faced terrible punishments as a result of Moloch or Baal's wrath. However, as I discussed in the chapter on suffering, many people still—like in ancient times—prioritize consumption, pleasure, and power above all else in their lives. In a sense, they are very religious in their devotion to these pursuits. Many even kill for them, though they certainly don't consider it a sacrifice to Baal, Moloch, or any other evil intellect.

Personally, I consciously choose not to serve or even please any evil intellect, whether explicitly or implicitly, real or fictional. However, when it comes to the existence of such an intellect, I must admit that the countless people who believe in it—either openly or subconsciously—and the significant tangible effects of their belief that I observe around me lead me to wonder: Does the evil intellect, in some sense, qualify as existing after all?

The line between existing and fictional may simply come down to how we define these terms. Even if we classify evil intellects as fictional, we cannot dismiss them lightly with a relaxed smile on our faces, as their effects in the world are undeniably real.

III. There are also many people who perceive God as a form of energy. However, since energy represents the capacity to perform work, such a God would undoubtedly be detectable through scientific experiments. If He were not detectable, it would imply that He has ceased participating in the world—perhaps right after creation—in which case His energy would have already been depleted. Alternatively, His power (energy expended per second) would be so minimal that He would be virtually powerless.

As Ratzinger puts it:

A god who cannot act is not God.

We could also equate God with matter itself, implying that he would be the sum of all energy contained within matter. In that case, Marxists would be right, and the world would be doomed to descend into a struggle between the strong and the weak, as previously discussed.

These *energy scenarios* remain plausible only if we dismiss all contrary evidence as mere coincidence—particularly if we assume, as an
axiom, that all randomness in the world is nothing more than meaningless noise. Many scientists take this stance, and I can't help but sense a
degree of fanaticism from some of them.

Personally, I choose not to believe in the concept of 'God as energy'.
When multiple plausible explanations exist, and none can be definitively
refuted by evidence, it is reasonable to believe and act according to the
one that does not lead to nihilism and destruction—even if, at first, it
seems less probable than the others. After all, how likely is it that the
guillotine will one day become a universal symbol of love? Yet the same
transformation occurred with the cross—an execution device that now
adorns ambulances worldwide as a symbol of saving lives (salvation)
and healing. The mechanism of a miracle lies in making an impression
on people through extreme improbability. Is there any other religion
where similarly unlikely 'transformations' have objectively occurred?

At what point does a coincidence become too unlikely to be dismissed
as mere chance? If you had 100 sheep, you might gamble on statistics
and accept losing a few. But with only one life, if you decide all is lost,
then it truly is.

IV. Ancient Greek philosophers developed another interesting concept of God, which they called 'logos' (meaning 'word' or 'reason'). While
difficult to explain directly, we can benefit from our software analogy
and think of 'logos' as akin to the source code of the universe—the ideal
source code that we can strive to uncover through intellectual efforts,
as previously discussed. Somehow, these Greek philosophers regarded
this source code as more real than the reality instantiated based on it.
Ratzinger describes this concept as the 'God of the Philosophers.' The
Greeks saw 'logos' as an abstract, detached, supreme intellect or Being,
but not a personal God capable of communication. Despite this, the idea
of 'logos' profoundly influenced early Christianity, as it represented the
closest concept to the Christian God among existing options. Over time,
'logos' became central to the development of both science and Catholic
theology.

Ratzinger writes:

> The Christian faith has—as we have seen—opted for the God
> of the philosophers over the gods of religions, that is, against

the myth of custom and solely for the truth of Being itself. This process gave rise to the accusation against the early Church that its followers were atheists. This charge arose from the fact that the early Church rejected the entire world of ancient religion, declaring none of it acceptable, but instead dismissing it entirely as an empty custom that stood in opposition to the truth.

(...)

The God we encounter here appears to us—much like in many texts of the Old Testament [of the Bible]—highly anthropomorphic, highly unphilosophical; he has passions like a human being—he rejoices, he seeks, he waits, he goes forth to meet others. He is not the unfeeling geometry of the universe [like Logos], nor the neutral justice that stands above all things, untouched by a heart and its emotions. Rather, he has a heart; he stands before us as a lover, with all the strangeness of one who loves.

People have been remarkably inventive in choosing what they place on a pedestal, worshiping it either explicitly or implicitly as their God. Mapping out the full spectrum of possible deities and commenting on each would be an overwhelming task. I'm a software engineer, not a professional in this area. However, I can say that in this chapter, we've discussed two concepts of God so far: One that cannot be worshipped and must be fought by all available means, and another that lacks any compelling reason to be worshipped or even believed to be real.

Some people have already, consciously or unconsciously, decided which God or deity they place their faith in. Many others, however, have yet to make such a decision. Some may be unwilling to invest significant effort into this crucial choice, while others see no compelling reason to approach the question at all. I certainly don't blame them—contemporary resources offering precise reasoning and logical clarity on this subject are surprisingly scarce. As a result, many people improvise daily, continually deciding which god or God to elevate in their lives. Catholics are in a somewhat similar situation, but with one key difference: We have been given, and have accepted, compelling reasons to turn toward faith in the Lord Jesus. This has always happened because someone loved us enough to guide us along that path. Consequently, our missteps now bear greater significance.

²⁴For, as it is written, "The name of God is blasphemed among the
        Gentiles because of you."   **Romans 2:24 (ESV)**

V. There is still one more concept of God we will address by revisiting our thought experiment from the previous chapter. Let's call this concept the 'Cosmic God,' or perhaps more fittingly, the 'God of Scientists.'
In this context, Ratzinger cites Albert Einstein:

> Einstein repeatedly rejects the concept of a personal God as 'anthropomorphic', associating it with the 'religion of fear' and 'moral religion', which he contrasts with what he sees as the only appropriate alternative: Cosmic religiosity. For him, this manifests as "ecstatic wonder at the harmony of natural law," in a "deep faith in the reason of the universe's structure," and in the "longing to comprehend, even if only a faint glimmer of the reason revealed in this world."

Einstein, along with many other prominent scientists, was captivated by the elegant, rational architecture they encountered in their fields of study. To them, the existence of a supreme intellect responsible for the logos underpinning the universe seemed far more plausible than the notion that all the intelligibility they observed was a result of mere chance—an accidental byproduct of their exploration. However, in their view, this wonderful supreme being they intuited behind such awe-inspiring elegance would surely regard humanity as insignificant—mere primitive specks of dust inhabiting one of the countless small planets. They believed this supreme being would be entirely indifferent to something as undeveloped as mankind.

Since this perspective remains widely held by many today, let's consider how *I am* might feel about it by taking our thought experiment even a step further. Let's engage in a speculative conversation with Him (the italicized text below represents my direct speech to God—a kind of prayer).

But first, imagine once more that you exist in a void—nothing is present. There is no earth, no stars, no physical laws, and no personal history of yours. It's just you and your creative potential. You are on the brink of creating this world. What is certain is that you will weave mathematics and geometry into it, crafting an architectural masterpiece of beauty and order. But could it be that you have no idea how awestruck we will be one day when we finally perceive the logos behind the elegance you have designed?

Therefore let me ask You, God:

Are You really so entirely other that we will never truly grasp anything about You? Obviously, besides all the laws of physics and the whole scientific endeavor and mathematics, logic, and related areas of exploration? I'm also ignoring the Bible altogether here as if it didn't exist.

So, let me correct myself a little bit. Is it just Your motives, God, that will forever elude our understanding so that we will never be able to act according to Your will? Putting the Bible aside again for a moment, I even dare to ask: Is Your will a void concept after all? In that case, dear God, You exist, but You indeed remain indifferent to us, leaving us to wrestle with Your creation as we see fit—subject to the rule of the strong over the weak. It means we are back to the violent clash of Marxist intellects, aren't we?

This is the end of the conversation for me for I cannot accept this! This God is apparently too great to be good. Without evidence, I refuse to live in that kind of world. I will always resist such misery, fighting it with every fiber of my being. Without evidence, my scientifically driven mind will never accept the possibility that God's motivation will forever remain completely beyond our understanding.

Now, allow me to respond to God based on what we discussed in the chapter on suffering:

If there is one most important conclusion from my private baby-like research so far, dear God, it's that—on this still somewhat unfamiliar planet—we are cared for with love most of the time of our lives, and the more, the closer we get to the rule of truth—to You, God. Is this love merely a byproduct of Your existence, something You are totally indifferent to and You perhaps didn't even consider? Am I to believe this? I refuse. And I didn't even need to turn to the Bible—which obviously speaks to the contrary.

A more plausible explanation, at least to me, is that You, God, not only knew but also willed it. When You existed in the void, before the world was created, You perhaps already had that intention in mind to design it a way that would allow You to share Yourself with beings like us—humans—and enable us to understand You, at least in part.

Dear God, why did You desire to create other free, independent beings capable of understanding You, even if only partially? I am asking since You apparently designed us with such independence that even merely acknowledging Your existence is our individual act of will rather than an undeniable conclusion drawn from some clear, irrefutable evidence.

Wouldn't this imply that we are, in some sense, Godomorphic beings rather than You being an anthropomorphic God? As expected, the word of God gives us some justification:

²⁷ So God created mankind in his own image,
   in the image of God he created them;
   male and female he created them.   **Genesis 1:27 (NIV)**

But let me continue:

Dear God, I undeniably feel Your love and care, as I have previously testified. It is just my personal experience, but I also haven't shared my life closely with anyone who has not had a similar experience. Am I to believe that You intentionally raised us, humans, to partially understand You, yet the love we feel from You is merely accidental and unintended—a misconception on our part? Admittedly, I haven't lived with those suffering in extreme conditions, and perhaps their testimony would differ—though I doubt it, given the many testimonies I've heard to the contrary.

This is the end of the speech.

Yet before we move on, it's worth reiterating that sharing life with other people in a family or community is an experience of a wholly different quality from merely hearing someone's testimony. Intellectuals often completely miss this point.

Living with my wife, for example, is entirely different from reading an article in which someone, somewhere, shares their testimony about marriage. The latter is always somewhat philosophical, while the former is always the truth to some extent. The latter is like reading about the laws of physics in a textbook, while the former is like conducting experiments to witness those laws in action—or perhaps even risking your life in a device you built upon the very principles you once studied in theory.

This kind of hands-on experience, which most engineers possess to some degree, is glaringly absent in many twentieth-century philosophers and theologians. Too often, they base their sweeping theories on *common knowledge* of science gleaned from newspapers. In any field, there inevitably comes a moment of confidence after you've grasped the basics—much like feeling assured after driving your first hundred miles. Ironically, that is the moment when you are most prone to a crash. In theology, this is when people suddenly feel emboldened to make sweeping interventions—such as attempting to *demystify* the Catholic faith by separating Christ from Jesus to align with *what we all know today science tells us.*

This, of course, was not the case with Albert Einstein. While he rejected the randomness inherent in quantum physics, he also couldn't accept his anthropomorphic Jewish God. Both views likely stemmed from the same root cause—Einstein's deep desire to reduce belief to a mere temporary stop on the path to calculable certainty, even if only a 'faint glimmer' of it, to borrow his own words. The Cosmic God could have provided that—if He existed. However, I argue that calculable certainty is the opposite of Love. Let's return to our thought experiment to find out why.

Imagine once more that you exist in a void. You stand on the brink of creation. Soon, there will be beings capable of partially understanding You. You will be their God, offering them love and care as parents do for their children. Given Your deep affection for these little creatures, it might seem natural for You to be present among them in an unquestionable way. Yet you choose to remain almost hidden. Why?

Let me engage in a prayer again:

Dear God, You act indirectly; You give care through the means of society, and You speak through prophets. As Ratzinger puts it, You approach man only through man; You seek out man in no other way but in his fellow humanity, perhaps with the exception of nature's sublime wonders. Why don't You just simply appear in all your glory? You would undoubtedly scare everyone to death, and those who wouldn't die on the spot would instantly stand up for whatever You stand up for and follow Your will at all times. Wouldn't this be the true kingdom of God? Why don't You like this kind of idea?

I think it is provable beyond doubt that God doesn't like this idea at all. The only plausible explanation I can see is that He desires genuine love from us, not mere fear. By designing the world this way, He grants us complete freedom to choose whether to place Him above all else in our lives—or even to believe in His existence at all. We are free to make misguided choices and to live as if He does not exist. Consequently, God cannot be present among us in an overt and undeniable way, which leads to suffering.

Not all suffering, of course, is the result of poor choices made by us or our neighbors. Illnesses and natural disasters, many of which we likely have no hand in causing, also bring about great suffering. If God truly loves us, why does He subject us to such suffering, especially when it seems that He designed the very forces that cause it?

It's clear that illnesses and natural disasters serve a crucial regulatory function in the environment, and they are necessary for the planet to sustain life and evolve. Animals also suffer, as they often fall prey to others—a fate from which we are largely exempt. But why can't God spare us from all other forms of suffering? If God truly loves us, wouldn't the ideal scenario be to make us the only creatures immune to all illnesses, floods, earthquakes, and fires—ensuring such disasters miraculously bypassed us? Of course, I refer only to illnesses, floods, and fires that we did not cause ourselves. So why didn't God design the world this way?

I believe any software engineer can deduce the most plausible reason: This approach would be exactly as unclean as writing additional complicated code to handle contingencies for everything that could go wrong, as we discussed in an earlier chapter. It would turn the world into a designer's nightmare. Such a design would not be worth entering the breathtaking elegance of Logos, the source code of this world. It would appear chaotic and inconsistent, an incomprehensible mess. It could render science nearly impossible, much like an overabundance of miracles would.

However, one could argue that if humans were responsible for writing software on which lives depend, we would go to great lengths to account for every possible contingency. Even if it meant overloading the code with countless if-else statements or hard-coded constants, ensuring safety would take precedence over elegance. So why, then, would a loving God prioritize elegant design over comprehensive safeguards?

The answer is that human lives are saved not by maximizing their earthly duration or minimizing suffering but by aligning them with God before death, as we will demonstrate in the second part of the book. If the world were an inconsistent mess, devoid of discernible order, people would struggle to understand who God is or to form a relationship with Him. They struggle with this challenge even in a world designed with geometric order and rational comprehensibility.

But isn't God supposed to be omnipotent, able to achieve all things simultaneously, without compromise, many may ask?

What an incredibly frustrating question for any software designer! We are all intimately familiar with the exasperation when someone—usually a manager who is entirely ignorant of all the complexities of system design—comes to us with a differently worded question that essentially asks the same.

This is how God responds to Job in a similar context in the book of Job (excerpts from a much longer speech):

2 Who is this that obscures my plans
    with words without knowledge?
3   Brace yourself like a man; I will question you,
    and you shall answer me.
4   Where were you when I laid the earth's foundation?
    Tell me, if you understand.
5   Who marked off its dimensions? Surely you know!
    Who stretched a measuring line across it?
6   On what were its footings set, or who laid its cornerstone
7   while the morning stars sang together
    and all the angels shouted for joy?   **Job 38:2–7 (NIV)**

39 Do you hunt the prey for the lioness
    and satisfy the hunger of the lions
40   when they crouch in their dens or lie in wait in a thicket?
41   Who provides food for the raven
    when its young cry out to God
    and wander about for lack of food?   **Job 38:39–41 (NIV)**

1 Do you know when the mountain goats give birth?
    Do you watch when the doe bears her fawn?
2   Do you count the months till they bear?
    Do you know the time they give birth?
3   They crouch down and bring forth their young;
    their labor pains are ended.
4   Their young thrive and grow strong in the wilds;
    they leave and do not return.   **Job 39:1–4 (NIV)**

Let us take a moment to examine the biblical book of Job. Job is a righteous man who loves God. After living a meaningful and prosperous life, he is suddenly struck by a series of devastating tragedies that shatter his entire world. He loses all his property and livestock, his children die, and he falls gravely ill. His suffering seems senseless, and Job cries out to God in resignation, overcome by despair and sorrow.

When his friends arrive, instead of offering comfort and admitting their own confusion about Job's situation, they admonish Job for his harsh words toward God. They insist that God is just, punishes only the wicked, and is always worthy of worship. They assume that Job must be at fault, urging him to repent for any past sins and to stop speaking against God.

Feeling betrayed by both his friends and God, Job struggles to understand what wrongdoing could have led to such profound suffering. He begins to question the fundamental order of the world and God's role in its design. Finally, God speaks to Job from within a whirlwind.

VI. The story of Job also helps us identify the final false god we must confront—a god so anthropomorphic and transactional that He reduces Himself to a mere caricature. This is the god I remember well from my childhood, when many in my country mocked Catholic beliefs. We might call him the 'God of Communists.' This is the same god Soviet astronaut Yuri Gagarin famously declared he did not see in space during his first journey to orbit, proclaiming his observation smugly as if it validated Marxist ideology.

Gagarin lived on the top happily thereafter for a while until another stronger intellect had him shut down from the sky while he was flying his fighter jet.

Thousands of years ago, biblical Job, unlike Gagarin, did not expect God to have a body; in fact, he didn't anticipate God being as transactional or capricious as Job's friends suggested. Job sought one thing only from God: For the events in his life to make sense and hold meaning. And ultimately, the story has a happy ending. Job was ultimately vindicated by God.

When you make the profound decision to place your faith in God based on personal experience and resolve that He alone is worthy of your worship, you cannot simply revert to Moloch or Marx if He disappoints you. In fact, if you fall into despair and resignation in your faith in Him, you have nowhere else to turn. You cannot revert to believing in self-deceptions of the Original Sin once you have abundant evidence at hand proving them to be falsehoods.

Nothing remotely comparable to Job's trials has happened to me, yet I have found myself crying the exact same things to God about God. It happened to me several times when I struggled to find meaning in the events of my life as well as in some events in the lives of other people. This may be the most difficult challenge for any believer in God. Job's story is harrowing, and only after thousands of years can we see how fruitful his suffering was for billions of other people, providing insights like the ones we briefly discussed here. One cannot always expect to grasp the meaning of the trials endured in this lifetime.

To summarize this chapter, God is not anthropomorphic; He cannot be viewed as such, like if viewed *from above.*

God created us in His own image—we are 'godomorphic' beings, yet God is not anthropomorphic. It's like a projection in geometry—you can't hope to understand all dimensions of something when you see just its mere projection to your humanly plain.

14

Trinitarian Design

In this chapter, we will take our thought experiment a step further and delve into the initial stages of creating the world. This chapter will be more speculative than the previous ones, as it explores concepts that have never been tested. Joseph Ratzinger also ventures into speculative territory when discussing the Holy Trinity in his book. I encourage you to approach this chapter with caution, mindful of its speculative nature and the potential for errors or misinterpretations.

In scientific exploration, certain questions remain unanswered because they are inherently excluded from the scope of investigation. These often involve concepts such as beauty, morality, and the nature of good and evil—each potentially being part of logos. As Ratzinger notes:

> The mathematician discovers the mathematics of the cosmos, the thought-ness of things. But nothing more. He discovers only the God of the philosophers.
>
> But is that really surprising? Can a mathematician, who views the world mathematically, find anything in the universe other than mathematics? Should we not rather ask him whether he has ever looked at the world in any way other than mathematically?

Ratzinger's observation is valid; however, there remains one fundamental question that science has grappled with yet cannot answer: Consciousness.

How is it that certain organisms—viewed as biological machines from a scientific perspective—possess consciousness? How does it arise?

Consider a scenario where we create a computer program that mimics human thought and behavior so convincingly that it passes a test (the well known 'Turing test'), making it indistinguishable from a biological human. Should we then regard this program as a conscious person, deserving of human rights? If it behaves in every way like a genuine human being, should we consider it a living entity endowed with intelligent consciousness and the dignity that comes with it?

But what if, later on, we discover a flaw—a minor imperfection that suggests the program may be just a simulation of the human mind? Does that give us the right to treat it as a mere object again? Can we simply switch it off as a thing? And what if, after shutting it down, we realize we were mistaken—that what we saw as proof of artificiality was actually a defining trait of a different form of intelligent life?

Questions like this, though they may sound like science fiction, point to a deeper issue: The current scientific model may simply not be powerful enough to adequately address them. I argue that this dilemma is ultimately a false one—born from the constraints of our scientific methods rather than from the fundamental nature of consciousness itself, which we will explore later.

Certain philosophical theories approach the question of consciousness from a different angle, positing that consciousness is something primordial to this world. Some philosophers go as far as to argue that only one's own consciousness truly exists, while other people are merely biological machines—devoid of consciousness, much like inanimate objects. Some theories extend this idea further, proposing that the material world itself is merely an illusion within one's own consciousness.

Consider the Turing test again: Even if you were to apply it to two biological humans and find no practical evidence that one of them is a simulated being, it still wouldn't prove that either of them possesses consciousness. The test only demonstrates indistinguishability in behavior, not the presence of consciousness.

The belief that others possess consciousness is so deeply ingrained that doubting it is often seen as a sign of mental impairment rather than an alternative philosophical perspective. The same holds true about the view that the material world is just an illusion. The truth is, there is no definitive way to refute these unconventional views through science or any other form of reasonably indisputable evidence. The belief that others have consciousness and that we share an objective reality is, ultimately, just that—a belief.

Similarly, I believe in God; you may not. Yet, no one would consider either belief grounds for hospitalization in a mental health institution. Yet in my country, people were once hospitalized and tortured for the former, while in the Middle Ages, people were once tortured and killed for the latter since it seemed an equally lunatic, dangerous idea for society.

Today, viewing other people as biological machines devoid of consciousness is considered a lunatic idea posing a significant danger to society since those who hold such a belief might begin to treat others more or less as mere objects, not as living beings with inherent dignity. I acknowledge this happens anyway, even without such lunatics. However, I argue it's due to the suboptimal model through which we interpret the world. If we saw humans primarily as consciousness in whom the Holy Spirit resides—rather than mere biological machines where consciousness somehow randomly emerged—it would be far more difficult to treat women as mere objects, for instance.

I once heard of a Catholic woman who thwarted a rape attempt by shouting, "I am a temple of the Holy Spirit." The attacker, struck by her words, immediately lost all desire and fled.

For the record, I firmly believe in the existence of an objective material world that we all share, as well as in the consciousness of others, just as I believe in my own. However, we must acknowledge that, at their core, these are beliefs. Isn't it high time—one may ask—to set aside the arrogance of the past few centuries and recognize that our views of the world are grounded in beliefs, not in the possession of truths?

In my alma mater's Theoretical Physics course, in the first lesson, we were taught that we hold these *beliefs*: We *believe* the laws of physics we've discovered were the same yesterday, hundreds, thousands, and even billions of years ago—and we also *believe* they will remain the same tomorrow, next year, and for millennia to come. I share that *belief* and consider it an elegant design.

The truth is that, despite all our efforts to understand it, we have no idea how consciousness originates. But what if consciousness never originated at all? What if it exists beyond time—always present, primordial to this world?

But how, then, do we explain the countless conscious beings who live and die, whose consciousness appears and then seemingly vanishes? Is there a model that can encompass all of this and provide a more comprehensive explanation?

I believe there is: The model of the Holy Trinity.

Let's return to our thought experiment. Imagine once again that you exist in a void, on the verge of creating the world. It's just you—your consciousness. You are who you are, unchanging.

Without change, there is no time—time doesn't exist because time cannot exist without change. Yet your consciousness exists! To grasp this, it's crucial to understand what Einstein's correction to the Newtonian model of space and time implied. Einstein argued that time cannot exist without a physical clock to measure it, just as distance has no meaning without a physical meter. Measuring distance purely by thought without a physical meter is as nonsensical as measuring time without an existing clock. Meters and clocks are subject to limitations, such as the speed of light, and can behave differently in various conditions, which means that time and space can be deformed—they are not absolute or uniform.

In the state where you simply *are*, time and space do not exist, yet your consciousness does. Your consciousness is primordial. If you claimed to have existed in this state for a billion years within an infinite cosmos, your words would be meaningless—merely a sound without substance.

Time begins the moment you set out to design the world. Where do you start?

Your vision is love. You intend to create free beings—free like yourself—whom you can love and care for. You seek to craft a world where, over time, these beings can come to understand love—you—so deeply that they might truly love you in return, without sacrificing their freedom. The more they understand you, the more they will become like you, and the more deeply they will be able to love you. This is your plan.

Science plays a vital role in this endeavor, which is why you intend to design the world as intelligible, consistent, and elegant. It will be a breathtaking design masterpiece, inspiring awe in your people from the very beginning. You wish to be their God, their Father, living as close to them as possible, involved in every aspect of their lives. No detail will be too small for your attention because, as God, you have no limits. Ratzinger, in this context, cites Hölderlin:

> "Non coerceri maximo, contineri tamen a minimo, divinum est": Not to be encompassed by the greatest, but to allow oneself to be encompassed by the smallest—that is divine.

So, you begin by designing quarks, leptons, and bosons, don't you? Of course not! That would be like beginning an intricate software project by first coding generic serializers for XML or JSON—before even defining the domain model and the fundamental high-level structures that shape the entire system. Just as an architect wouldn't begin by designing a flat's electrical wiring before determining its layout and purpose, you must first establish the overarching design and principles before addressing the specifics of elementary particles. You never begin with low-level details; they must be designed to serve the high-level vision.

This is how the word of God describes the initial design process:

¹ In the beginning God created the heaven and the earth.
² And the earth was without form and void,
and darkness was upon the face of the deep.
And the Spirit of God moved upon the face of the waters.
³ And God said, "Let there be light"; and there was light.
⁴ And God saw the light, that it was good;
and God divided the light from the darkness.

Genesis 1:1–4 (KJ21)

The full text appears at the beginning of the Bible. These lines describe the first moments of *time* when change occurs. However, I argue that all of this took place before the Big Bang. This is akin to writing the initial blocks of code—defining fundamental types and classes, and outlining the core concepts that will shape the world. This is logos. Yet, many steps remain before execution—before the Big Bang.

However, the fundamental setting is already taking shape: Light, which structures space and time; matter, water, and the periodic cycles of day and night; oceans, land, atmosphere, and green plants sprouting from seeds. The stars and celestial bodies will serve as markers of space and time in the future. More importantly, they will offer insight into the past deeds of Providence:

¹⁴And God said,
> Let there be lights
> in the expanse of the heavens
> to separate the day from the night,
> and let them be
> signs and tokens [of God's provident care],
> and [to mark] seasons, days, and years.   **Genesis 1:14 (AMPC)**

According to Scripture, God next defined the animals, providing them with plants for food. Finally, He created humans, entrusting them with the role of caretakers over creation—a somewhat similar role God has Himself. At the culmination of creation, God introduced the concept of the sacred by sanctifying the seventh day—setting it apart as holy. We will explore this theme further later on.

Once God established what we might describe in AI terms as the 'logos fitness function,' He unleashed the chaos—the Big Bang—initiating a process that evolves the world autonomously according to the constraints given by logos. This selective process possesses the advantage of backward intelligibility, enabling us to trace the development of creation—much like reviewing commits in God's divine source control, so to speak. Everything we need to know is present, yet God can remain hidden.

More precisely, it should be said that God was not always hidden. God withdrew into hiding after the first man endowed with free will—'Adam' (whose name means 'man')—committed the first sin. This took place when Adam and his wife, Eve, ate from the Tree of the Knowledge of Good and Evil, which God had expressly forbidden. Had their love for God been perfect, they would not have defied His will; instead, they would have upheld what He stands for. However, even the very first human succumbed to temptation by the evil intellect, rebelling against God almost immediately. As a result, God expelled Adam and Eve from the state of existence in which His presence had been direct, unquestionable, and permanent—removing them 'from the Garden of Eden'.

But let us now return to the creative process of God. The world, as I experience it, fills me with awe. Its inherent beauty and elegance leave me breathless. I also deeply admire the elegance of the logos—some of which has been revealed through science and preserved in books. I say all of this not to sound disrespectful when I also say that the creative process I've just described is quite familiar to software engineers. In fact, it closely parallels approaches that many of us use throughout our professional lives. If I were to design something akin to this world—albeit on a far less complex scale—I would likely follow steps similar to those I ascribe to God in this chapter. Rather than constructing it atom by atom, I would define fundamental rules and let the *landscape* take shape iteratively through a partially random, self-organizing process.

I can imagine Joseph Ratzinger asking: *Is this really surprising? Can a software engineer, perceiving the world through the lens of software design, see anything other than software engineering in the universe?* Naturally, the answer is no. But when mathematicians and physicists do this, society tends to accept it as nothing but the truth. I'm afraid I will not be as lucky.

I dream of *coding the world again*—of constructing a detailed, elegant, and precise understanding of the logos and of God, mirroring the true logos as faithfully as possible. This could be a deeply collaborative endeavor, where—alongside current science—entire monasteries could dedicate themselves to capturing the nuances of our inner lives: Morality, education, aesthetics, the beauty of spiritual music (such as that composed by Bach), and much more. With coding, we are not limited by the level of detail; we can immerse ourselves in even the smallest of things—an act that, as we read, is divine.

Reading an elegant codebase that conveys morality is nothing like enduring a diatribe from a moralizing speaker whose harsh words obscure the love of God, reducing it to a cold, mechanistic process devoid of grace. In code, there is no speaker—only the reader, who engages in interpretation. Any understanding reached is personal, not one imposed by a detached orator. Few things are more needed in today's church than this.

However, it must be acknowledged that we cannot be like God. We cannot create another world like ours—not even a vastly simpler one. I argue there is at least one crucial thing we can never do. This limitation will also serve as undeniable proof that we don't exist in some bizarre simulation crafted by a humanoid being dwelling somewhere outside this world. Instead, it will affirm that we are, in fact, creatures directly facing God.

To explore what we can and cannot do, let's revisit our thought experiment. Imagine yourself at a moment in time when the world is fully formed, teeming with life—including primates—on Earth.

It is easy to envision 'hooking' your consciousness to any location, marveling at your creation without the need for a physical body—just as, in a computer simulation, one can observe the system's internal state from any point at any time, unbound by one's physical form.

Similarly, it's conceivable that you could choose to incarnate—bring your consciousness into the context of one of these primates. You could use its mouth to speak and its limbs to move. It would be akin to representing a character in a virtual reality. To project this concept even further, one might argue this is how you create something very similar to humans—a primate with consciousness. In this scenario, the consciousness would be God's, but it represents our closest approximation to creating humans we discussed so far.

Since you—as God—have complete control over time, you can pause and resume your 'world simulation' at will, seamlessly shifting between the perspectives of individual primates. Given that the number of these primates is finite, you can incarnate within each of them, experiencing their lives moment by moment—sequentially ordered within your singular consciousness of God. In this way, you can live as many of their lives as you desire, experiencing every detail with the utmost closeness.

At this stage, such a scenario remains within the realm of possibility for a highly sophisticated computer simulation designed by skilled engineers. Though we would not achieve the same level of beauty, complexity, and elegance, it is feasible. However, in such a simulated world, genuine love remains unattainable. For love to become possible, God would need to take a step back, allowing only a small fragment of His consciousness—the inner voice of the Holy Spirit—to remain perceptible in these primates while otherwise granting complete freedom to the thus newly created 'Individuals.'

If God can 'lend' His consciousness to a primate while relinquishing control, He has, in effect, created a human person. This model does not contradict the current scientific understanding of the world; rather, it expands the existing framework by introducing the dimension of consciousness.

It is crucial to remember that a model should never be conflated with reality! The world is *not photons and atoms*; similarly, humans are *not primates to whom God lends his consciousness relinquishing his control.* However, while this new model may not fully capture how the world is 'implemented,' it seems to offer a more comprehensive explanation than the current scientific framework alone.

Perhaps God is not as similar to man as He appears in this new model. Likewise, modern computer architectures are far more powerful and elegant than the Turing Machine—their theoretical mathematical model—yet we still use it to understand computers.

Now consider this: One of the steps we've discussed cannot be replicated in a simulated computer environment. This step is the relinquishing of control—granting true freedom, which gives rise to a new human person, an individual. While we might attempt to mimic this by programming the simulated individual to act randomly on our watch within predefined bounds, genuine randomness would require an external input, like an antenna connecting to our physical world, as discussed in the chapter on randomness. Even in that case, the behavior would be autonomous yet ultimately devoid of true meaning or purpose—resulting in mere superficial freedom. Until someone proves this conclusion wrong—which is impossible in my view—we can rest confident that we do not live in a simulated computer environment but rather exist as beings directly facing God.

This also partially addresses the question of the Earth's age from a Biblical perspective. While Biblical Adam—the first free individual ever created—is estimated to have lived around six millennia ago, this does not mean the Earth itself is only several thousand years old. Rather, it suggests that the 'years of conscious human freedom' differ in nature from the 'years of iterative development required to evolve the world toward the logos fitness function optimum.' As a software engineer, I can simulate the latter on a computer—adjusting its speed faster or slower than my own perception of time—whereas the pace of the former remains beyond my control.

I am not suggesting that free-willed humans have existed for only six thousand years. Rather, I seek to highlight a specific moment when the first humanoid primate transitioned into the first true human—a transformation that may have occurred relatively recently.

The Catholic Creed, a central prayer encapsulating the core beliefs of the faith, proclaims belief in one God: The Father, the Son, and the Holy Spirit—one God in three persons. The first part of this book explores the Father (and, to a lesser extent, the Holy Spirit). The second part will center on the Son, the Lord Jesus, who is 'consubstantial with the Father'—fully human and fully divine.

In terms of our model:

The Son is the man in whom God the Father did not relinquish control of His consciousness.

It is evident that there can be only one God the Son, regardless of His bodily form, as His identity and will are inseparable from those of God the Father. One could say that God the Son is who God the Father has always been, even 'before' time. In the New Testament, St. Paul (possibly) refers to Christ appearing simultaneously to around 500 people in different locations. Even in this instance, Christ remains one.

The Catholic Creed expresses it as follows:

> I believe in one Lord Jesus Christ,
> the Only Begotten Son of God,
> born of the Father before all ages.

The new model also sheds light on the following part of the Creed:

> (...) he came down from heaven,
> and by the Holy Spirit
> was incarnate of the Virgin Mary,
> and became man.

It is also evident why the Holy Spirit speaks through the mouth of the Lord Jesus rather than solely through the inner voice within our own consciousness that comes from God the Father. For us, the inner voice can be suppressed or distorted by free will. However, in Jesus, He and the Father were always in complete harmony; thus, the voice of Jesus remains the pure and unaltered voice of the Holy Spirit. This theological concept, known as the 'Filioque,' was a significant factor in the schism between Eastern and Western Christianity:

> I believe in the Holy Spirit,
> the Lord, the giver of life,
> who proceeds from the Father and the Son (...).

In this context, Ratzinger cites the following passages from the Gospel of John, in which Jesus speaks about Himself:

³⁰I and the Father are one.   **John 10:30 (NIV)**

³⁰By myself I can do nothing;
    I judge only as I hear, and my judgment is just,
    for I seek not to please myself but him who sent me.
                                                            John 5:30 (NIV)

¹⁹Jesus gave them this answer:
    "Very truly I tell you,
    the Son can do nothing by himself;
    he can do only what he sees his Father doing,
    because whatever the Father does the Son also does.
²⁰ For the Father loves the Son and shows him all he does.
    Yes, and he will show him even greater works than these,
    so that you will be amazed.
²¹ For just as the Father raises the dead
    and gives them life, even so the Son gives life
    to whom he is pleased to give it.
²² Moreover, the Father judges no one,
    but has entrusted all judgment to the Son,
²³ that all may honor the Son just as they honor the Father.
    Whoever does not honor the Son
    does not honor the Father, who sent him."
                                                        John 5:19–23 (NIV)

A foundational Catholic dogma states that Christ Jesus possessed two wills: A human will and a divine will. Yet, when we speak of the perfect harmony between God the Father and God the Son, we affirm that the will and identity of the Son are inseparable from those of the Father. How can these truths be reconciled? Why is this distinction crucial to our understanding of faith and salvation?

In the second part of this book, we will examine Jesus as the ultimate role model for humanity. To fulfill this role, Jesus had to be fully and completely human during His time on earth. If He were fundamentally different from us—some other kind of being—how could we aspire to emulate Him? How could we strive to achieve His perfection in our earthly lives if He were beyond our nature? Such a difference would make His example incomprehensible and our hope unattainable.

But this raises profound questions: What was it like to be Jesus, in whom, according to our model, God the Father never relinquished control of His consciousness? For instance, why did Jesus, before His arrest and crucifixion, pray to the Father to "take this bitter cup from Me" if His divine will was perfectly aligned with the Father's? Also, why did the devil tempt Jesus in the wilderness, knowing the attempt was futile? Could Jesus have disobeyed the Father? Is His ultimate merit found in the fact that He chose obedience? Did this obedience serve as the decisive factor in humanity's salvation?

Moreover, how does Jesus differ in this respect from His mother, the Virgin Mary, who has also always been revered by the Church for having never disobeyed God's will? Can Jesus and Mary be compared in their perfect submission to the Father? If so, does this risk obscuring Christ's unique nature, as Protestants often caution? Might they have a valid point in warning against potential deviations from the true image of God in Catholic theology?

If we believe that Jesus was fully one of us, we should be able to find analogies in our own lives that reflect His experience of possessing two wills. These analogies could help us empathize more deeply with Jesus in this regard. The similarity between Jesus and Mary suggests that such a parallel may indeed exist.

One analogy that resonates deeply with me and helps me envision Jesus' experience is that of a God-given mission. Many of us believe that God has entrusted us with a mission. One of the most profound examples is the calling to become a mother or father. Other God-given missions might include a call to kingship, the priesthood, or religious life.

The Bible provides numerous examples of individuals called to God-given missions. These transitions are often marked by the bestowal of a new name, symbolizing that while we remain the same person physically, we are fundamentally transformed. Our lives are irrevocably changed in a profound way, though not at the atomic level.

The most universal transformation in the Christian life occurs at baptism, where we receive a name signifying our belonging to Christ. Another example is the sacrament of confirmation, in which we adopt the name of a patron saint, emphasizing our specific Christian mission.

Similarly, in the Bible, individuals sent on significant missions often received new names to signify their new roles. Abram became Abraham, Sarai became Sarah, Jacob became Israel, Simon became Peter, and Saul became Paul. Such renaming highlights the profound transformation in identity and purpose that accompanies a divine calling.

Being sent on a mission transforms your perspective, broadening your view of the world. You begin to see not only from your personal vantage point but also through the lens of your mission. For example, as a parent, you perceive the world not just as an individual but as a guardian responsible for a family. As a leader, you view life through the responsibilities of overseeing a kingdom or the Church. This dual perspective is inherent in every God-given mission and often brings tension.

Your personal desires often clash with the responsibilities of a mission. In many situations, you might have willed something quite different if you were acting solely as an individual rather than as someone entrusted with a God-given mission. At this point, your individuality and mission become inseparable—united, much like Jesus and Christ. If you are a parent, even if you were to deny or neglect your role, your mistakes would not make you any less of a parent.

This union does not imply two separate persons within one body. The same was true for Jesus, and likewise for Mary.

So what, then, were the differences?

Both Jesus and Mary were like us, yet their origins differ fundamentally. Like all of us, the Virgin Mary's individuality was created by God. In contrast, Jesus' individuality was never created. Despite these differences, neither Jesus nor Mary could act against their own will—just as we cannot.

This distinction highlights a profound truth: Mary, being fully human, had the ability to will against God because she was not divine. Yet she freely and wholeheartedly chose to align her will with God's, embracing her mission as the Mother of God.

Jesus, being fully divine and fully human, could not act against God's will, for He is God and cannot will against Himself. Thus, His divine will is perfectly united with the Father's, and His actions flow from this unity, much like a parent's actions—whether good or bad—flow from their identity as a parent. Of course, in Jesus' case, His identity as God meant that His will was always love—never anything less.

If we worship Jesus for never acting against God's will, we are ultimately worshipping Him for embodying exactly what the early Church believed Mary to be.

Mary deserves profound reverence for her willing acceptance of her God-given mission, through which our salvation became possible. Through her free will, she became the Mother of God, fulfilling a pivotal role in the divine plan. Yet God the Son deserves the highest reverence, for He is the eternal Creator of the universe.

In this sense, Protestant thinkers are both correct and mistaken. They are correct in affirming that Jesus deserves greater reverence than Mary. However, they may err in suggesting that greater reverence for Jesus necessitates diminishing honor for Mary.

True reverence for the Lord Jesus is not achieved by diminishing Mary's honor but by worshipping God for who He truly is—the singular source of unconditional love. This distinction is essential, for at stake is the true image of God.

When the devil tempted Jesus in the wilderness, his goal was to distort our understanding of God by presenting a false image—a God who could act against His own will.

In considering the events in the Garden of Gethsemane, it is important to remember that the apostles were asleep while Jesus prayed to the Father to take the bitter cup from Him. The scriptural account is not a verbatim transcript of that moment but rather Jesus' own accurate and comprehensible explanation of His actions while the apostles slept. Certainly, He did not intend to suggest that He could have acted contrary to the Father's will. He wanted to convey his fully human emotions and fears.

During their earthly lives, both Jesus and Mary shared our human nature, yet their differences were profound.

Mary was born like all of us and, at a pivotal moment, freely embraced her God-given mission. This has made her a person of utmost reverence and importance since the early Church. She is believed to have been gifted with the natural ability to see all the delusions stemming from Original Sin, yet she still could have opposed God. However, she chose to fully align her will with Him. That is why she remains immensely relatable in the Catholic tradition, despite the few mentions of her in the Bible.

In contrast, Jesus was not merely sent on a mission; He Himself is the mission—Love incarnate. At a specific moment in history, this eternal mission took on flesh, receiving a human body so that Jesus might dwell among us and make our salvation possible.

The profound and unexpected design solution lies in the fact that, despite God's fundamentally different origin, He truly and naturally became one of us—He found a way.

Thus far, we have explored the following parts of the Creed:

> I believe in one God, the Father almighty,
> maker of heaven and earth,
> of all things visible and invisible.
>
> I believe in one Lord Jesus Christ,
> the Only Begotten Son of God,
> born of the Father before all ages.
>
> (...) begotten, not made,
> consubstantial with the Father;
> through him all things were made.
>
> (...) he came down from heaven,
> and by the Holy Spirit
> was incarnate of the Virgin Mary,
> and became man.
>
> (...)
>
> I believe in the Holy Spirit,
> the Lord, the giver of life,
> who proceeds from the Father and the Son,
> (...),
> who has spoken through the prophets.
>
> (...)
>
> Amen.

At this point, I recommend reading the first part of Introduction to Christianity by Joseph Ratzinger, a recognized authority within the

Church. This will allow you to discern whether he conveys the same theological truths, albeit expressed differently—including his perspective on God's consciousness.

I hope I have clarified to some extent that *what we all know science tells us* should not be used to justify the perspective on the Lord Jesus that Joseph Ratzinger critiques in the following passage of his book:

> Instead of being the God who became man, Christ is reduced to merely someone who has experienced God in a special way. He is seen as an enlightened one and, thus, no longer fundamentally different from other enlightened figures, such as Buddha. However, in such an interpretation, the figure of Jesus loses its inner logic.

Let this passage serve as a reference point, for everything that follows would be incomprehensible without the coming of Christ Jesus.

Part II

Jesus of Nazareth

— 15 —

God's Desire

At the end of Part One, we introduced a software analogy to reconcile the existence of consciousness with the current scientific model. I argued that if consciousness is primordial to this world and God exists as the intellect behind all creation, then the most straightforward explanation for the design of the world is the existence of a single consciousness—the consciousness of God.

Also, I suggested that it is feasible to envision God defining the Logos—the source code of the universe—and using it as a fitness function to guide creation's evolution. This process unfolds in a way that is partially random and stochastic, yet remains intelligible and traceable in reverse. We also explored the experience of incarnation, which is still within the realm of human imagination—it's not difficult to imagine coding a virtual world and embodying an entity within that environment, experiencing the world from the entity's perspective, and interacting with that environment as that entity.

Let's take this idea further and imagine what it would feel like if the simulated entity you embody suddenly began exhibiting free will. In a virtual environment, this would be just a fascinating curiosity, as you wouldn't be seriously engaged in such a world—it wouldn't be real. But if something similar occurred in the real world, it would probably feel akin to someone suddenly taking control of your body—moving your limbs, speaking, walking, eating, and living your life *before your own eyes*. If this happened abruptly and without your consent, it would feel like a nightmare, as if your life had been stolen from you. However, if you willingly lent your consciousness and body to your own child—someone you love and deeply care for, placing your hopes in them—the experience of sharing your consciousness with them might be full of joy rather than suffering.

In fact, it could even become a deeply meaningful connection if your child freely and willingly chooses to act in ways you approve of because they deeply admire and cherish what you stand for. Because of your love for them, it might feel like a miracle to witness your child living the life you've always envisioned for them. If they love what you stand for, they love you (in the case of God, "who He is" and "what He stands for" are inseparable—one and the same).

However, if your child does not return your love, the situation could just as easily become a nightmare. Imagine if your child chooses to privatize and exploit your consciousness, using it for ends that you despise and condemn. Few things are more painful than the thought of your estranged child usurping your very consciousness.

If our model is accurate, acting against God is far more disrespectful and shamelessly arrogant than we can fathom. It's akin to being given shelter and repaying that kindness by setting it on fire for amusement, for momentarily escaping troubles while mocking the good person who helped you by providing it. It is as if you scoff at them, dismissing them as a naive idealist or a weak do-gooder—feeling, if only for a moment, as though you've transcended all creation. In your contempt, you behave as if God is absent—yet He witnesses everything firsthand, from within your very consciousness.

To illustrate this, consider the following passage of the Bible describing the events that took place beneath the cross after the crucifixion:

[35] The people stood watching,
and the rulers even sneered at him.
They said, "He saved others; let him save himself
if he is God's Messiah, the Chosen One."
[36] The soldiers also came up and mocked him.
They offered him wine vinegar
[37] and said, "If you are the king of the Jews, save yourself."
[38] There was a written notice above him, which read:
This Is The King Of The Jews.
[39] One of the criminals who hung there hurled insults at him:
"Aren't you the Messiah? Save yourself and us!"

Luke 23:35–39 (NIV)

I believe that if God suffered immensely, His greatest suffering was not in Christ Jesus' consciousness on the cross, nor was it due to physical pain or the anticipation of death. His suffering in Jesus' body was not nearly as great as the suffering He endured through the consciousness of those standing below the cross, watching. This passage continues the biblical account:

40 But the other criminal [hanging to the right of Jesus]
    rebuked him. "Don't you fear God," he said,
    "since you are under the same sentence?
41   We are punished justly,
    for we are getting what our deeds deserve.
    But this man has done nothing wrong."
42   Then he said, "Jesus, remember me
    when you come into your kingdom."
43   Jesus answered him,
    "Truly I tell you, today you will be with me in paradise."

Luke 23:40–45 (NIV)

This passage suggests that even last-minute remorse can be enough to tear down the barrier between oneself and the Truth. Sometimes, that is all it takes to be saved. We are all sinners, yet some fail to recognize any reason for remorse, nor do they show respect, compassion, or love for God, recognizing His presence.

However, if you do not genuinely seek the Truth, salvation remains unlikely—even if you refrain from murder and theft, as we will later explore. The true danger lies in believing yourself righteous when you are not—a trap that ensnares both believers and nonbelievers alike. As the Gospels reveal, the only thing that truly provokes Jesus'—and therefore God's—anger is the delusion of righteousness. Mistakes can be forgiven, but through ignorance and disrespect, you may sever yourself from God indefinitely.

In the passage above, God, through Jesus, forgives the sins of the murderer, who appears to be the only one genuinely seeking the truth about his life situation and capable of appreciating God's presence. To respect God's presence is to love Him, even if one is a great sinner. Conversely, to feel *OK* is to ignore His presence—for no one can feel *OK* before God.

Committing the grave sin of murder is one thing—you may deserve punishment, even death, for it. But it is an entirely different matter to spend years abusing the gift of free will, living selfishly and comfortably while disregarding God, as though He were absent from your very consciousness. To God, such disdainful ignorance may be far more appalling than sincere remorse for a single act of murder.

This perspective sheds light on the following Gospel passage, in which Jesus addresses a young man who professes to have followed all the Old Testament commandments:

21 Jesus answered, "If you want to be perfect,
go, sell your possessions and give to the poor,
and you will have treasure in heaven.
Then come, follow me."
22 When the young man heard this,
he went away sad, because he had great wealth.
23 Then Jesus said to his disciples,
"Truly I tell you, it is hard for someone who is rich
to enter the kingdom of heaven.
24 Again I tell you, it is easier for a camel
to go through the eye of a needle
than for someone who is rich
to enter the kingdom of God."
25 When the disciples heard this,
they were greatly astonished and asked,
"Who then can be saved?"
26 Jesus looked at them and said,
"With man this is impossible,
but with God all things are possible."

Matthew 19:21–26 (NIV)

Earlier in this book, we referenced Joseph Ratzinger's description of Judaism as 'the way of life.' This passage highlights the situation of adhering to religious practices while simultaneously misusing free will—leading a self-centered, complacent life that disregards the divine presence permeating our consciousness.

This temptation is particularly strong for the wealthy, yet the issue is not wealth itself, but one's attachment to it—refusing to follow Jesus because of it. Wealth often fosters a personal bubble of comfort, where one may give God what *one owes Him* and then pursue self-centered desires, believing oneself righteous while remaining detached from God.

Yet the true owner of all possessions, including our very consciousness, is God. Since all your resources belong to God, they should be used to fulfill His will. He entrusts you with their management—including your time—so that you may steward them as He would. By doing so, you will find life more meaningful, engaging, and fulfilling—beyond anything money can buy, whether through insurance policies, material pleasures, or vacations.

Even while on holiday, rest should serve to rejuvenate you, enabling you to pursue God's will more effectively upon your return. Jesus Himself, who had no private life apart from His service, embodies the idea that His identity and His actions are inseparable. The biblical passage above suggests that unless one aligns with this principle, salvation remains beyond reach.

The following few verses illustrate that disrespect toward God—who manifests in your consciousness as the voice of the Holy Spirit—surpasses all repentable sins:

[31] And so I tell you,
   every kind of sin and slander
   can be forgiven,
   but blasphemy against the Spirit
   will not be forgiven.
[32]   Anyone who speaks a word against the Son of Man
   will be forgiven,
   but anyone who speaks against the Holy Spirit
   will not be forgiven,
   either in this age or in the age to come.

Matthew 12:31–32 (NIV)

Ratzinger writes:

   The true statement of faith is this: With Jesus, the distinction between office and person ceases to exist; in his case, such a separation simply becomes irrelevant. He is his office, and his office is him. The two are inseparable. Here, there is no private realm, no reserved space for a private 'I' that stands apart from his actions and deeds—no moment when he is 'off duty.' The 'I' is the work, and the work is the 'I.'

Even within the faith's own self-understanding, as expressed in the Creed, Jesus did not leave behind a body of teachings that could be separated from his 'I,' as one might collect and appreciate the ideas of great thinkers without considering the person behind them. The Creed does not present a doctrine of Jesus; in fact, no one at the time even considered attempting such a thing—an idea that might seem obvious to us today—because their fundamental understanding of his identity pointed in an entirely different direction.

(...)

The one who gives himself wholly to the service of others—who embraces complete selflessness and self-emptying—becomes, in the fullest sense, Selflessness and Self-Emptying itself. And it is precisely such a person who embodies the true essence of humanity: The human being of the future, where the divine and the human are no longer separate but interwoven.

Expressed in terms of our software analogy:

If Christ Jesus is the man in whom God the Father retained full control of His consciousness, then for the rest of us, God desires that, out of sincere love and free will, we willingly return all control back to Him. Christ Jesus is the Logos made flesh—the ultimate truth of what humanity is meant to be 'in itself.' God seeks our true sonship. This means He desires each of us to become like Jesus as if born into our particular personal situations. In this way, we, as the Church, gradually evolve into the collective body of Christ—the fully realized Kingdom of God.

Earlier in this book, we referenced the powerful opening of the Gospel of John:

[1] In the beginning was the Word,
     and the Word was with God,
     and the Word was God.   **John 1:1 (NIV)**

A few verses later, the passage continues:

¹⁴The Word became flesh
and made his dwelling among us.
We have seen his glory,
the glory of the one and only Son,
who came from the Father,
full of grace and truth.   **John 1:14 (NIV)**

Christ Jesus acts like a fitness function, drawing humanity toward
God, the random element in it being our free will. In a way, this could
be seen as a continuation of the evolution of species. The underlying
process is similar and the method is the same.

Ratzinger articulates this concept as follows:

> If Jesus is the exemplary man, in whom the true form of hu-
> manity—God's idea of man—fully comes to light, then he
> cannot merely be an absolute exception, a curiosity in which
> God demonstrates to us what is possible. Rather, his exis-
> tence concerns all of humanity. The New Testament makes
> this clear by calling him an 'Adam'; in the Bible, this word
> expresses the unity of the entire human being, which is why
> one speaks of the biblical idea of a 'corporate personality.'

> If Jesus is called 'Adam,' this means that he is destined to
> gather the entire [collective] being of 'Adam' within himself.
> This, in turn, implies that the reality Paul refers to—though
> often incomprehensible to us today—as the 'Body of Christ'
> is an intrinsic necessity of his existence. He cannot remain
> an exception but must "draw all people to himself" (cf. John
> 12:32).

Here is the passage by St. Paul that Ratzinger references. In the
New Testament, Paul summarizes the shift from 'the way of life'—which
he calls 'the law' (as outlined in the Old Testament)—to faith in Christ
Jesus, where being 'in Christ' signifies belonging to His collective body.

²³Before the coming of this faith,
we were held in custody under the law,
locked up until the faith

that was to come would be revealed.
24 So the law was our guardian until Christ came
that we might be justified by faith.
25 Now that this faith has come,
we are no longer under a guardian.
26 So in Christ Jesus
you are all children of God through faith,
27 for all of you who were baptized into Christ
have clothed yourselves with Christ.
28 There is neither Jew nor Gentile,
neither slave nor free,
nor is there male and female,
for you are all one in Christ Jesus.   **Galatians 3:23–28 (NIV)**

Recognizing and acknowledging God's presence in the Body of Christ is not merely a matter of theological understanding; it is primarily a matter of skill, routine, and discipline.

For instance, it takes great effort to feel compassion for God suffering in a sinner before feeling repulsion or hatred for the evil they have brought into your life. If only I could improve at this, I might be able to explain the process (perhaps in a future book).

Undoubtedly, the foundation of this practice is prayer—establishing a regular prayer routine. It may be a prayer of compassion—such as for a sinner—or a plea for an end to war, both of which you and God suffer through and long to end. At times, God may not grant your requests, knowing what you do not—yet you can still pray, and in doing so, share His burden.

You can also seek guidance. In my experience, such prayers are almost always answered—often in unexpected ways.

You can thank God or marvel at His creation. No matter the form, prayer is a conversation with someone who is always present, even in an empty room. He is your closest person. How tragic it is to neglect the One who shares every moment of your life, as if He does not exist.

But even if you pray many times a day, you can stay detached from God. The wealthy young man is an example of this, but so is anyone who cannot forgive, holds onto grievances, or nurses wounded pride. Both unforgiveness and wealth can trap you in the same way—by keeping you focused on your own story rather than your role in God's.

— 16 —

Is he He?

So far, we have implicitly viewed Jesus of Nazareth as the Christ figure, but this assumption may hinder a deeper understanding. Let's explore this topic in greater depth.

At the outset of this book, we sought the truth about our personal circumstances. I argued that the closer we align with truth, the more we recognize it as the ultimate source of the love and care we experience in the world. This realization did not come from the Bible but rather from our own observations.

In the next step, we questioned whether life can truly hold meaning without acknowledging a higher intellect behind creation (behind the material world). We concluded that this intellect—God—quite possibly exists and loves us. Again, this conclusion was reached without invoking the word of God.

Finally, we arrived at the concept of a singular consciousness of God. We speculated that if God could relinquish control within His own consciousness, He might give rise to individuals—human beings. Even for this idea, we did not rely on Scripture.

Having developed this theory of God—arguably a scientific theory in the broadest sense—the next logical step is to examine human history for individuals in whom God retained full control of His consciousness. In simple terms, we are searching for individuals who, while fully human, were absolutely incapable of acting outside of God's will in anything they did. Such figures are of paramount importance because their lives may provide profound insight into who God is.

Even without expertise in world religions, we have ample resources (including AI models) to identify potential candidates for further study.

I encourage you to conduct your own research. In my private search, I found no individuals who meet the criteria, aside from Jesus of Nazareth. Even self-proclaimed Second Comings of Jesus failed to meet the criteria. I expected to find more candidates. While the presence of only one does not constitute definitive proof, it strongly suggests that Jesus of Nazareth stands apart and merits deeper examination.

The first question to consider is whether Jesus of Nazareth was a historical figure or a myth. While the vast majority of historians agree that Jesus was indeed a historical person, there is a minority who challenge this view. These scholars argue that contemporary evidence is sparse and that many elements of Jesus' story resemble earlier myths of dying-and-rising gods. This, they suggest, indicates that his life narrative may have been shaped by pre-existing religious motifs.

A fundamental challenge of historical science is its inability to directly observe or experiment with the past. For example, we cannot retroactively instruct Jesus to hire an independent biographer to document his every action.

The four Gospels are not firsthand contemporary accounts; they were composed more than 30 years after Jesus' death. During this period, early Christians faced intense persecution, and there was a genuine risk that firsthand witnesses—some of whom had known Jesus personally—might be killed before they could transmit their knowledge. This urgency likely motivated the preservation of oral traditions in written form.

Although this may sound facetious, it raises an intriguing question: If Jesus was truly divine, could he not have foreseen the future need for independent contemporary documentation? Interestingly, some historical events marked by significant divine intervention have left behind extensive contemporary documentation. One such case is St. Joan of Arc (who lived 1412 to 1431), whose extraordinary experiences were meticulously documented in judicial records from her trial and subsequent rehabilitation. Mark Twain's historical novel Personal Recollections of Joan of Arc draws from these detailed records, presenting a compelling narrative of divine involvement that is difficult to dispute.

Let's return to those who knew Jesus personally. Joseph Ratzinger has been criticized for relying too much on the Gospel of John in his writings. The Apostle John, whom Jesus (according to the Gospels) entrusted with the care of his mother Mary, was likely the only apostle to die of natural causes. He is believed to have died in Ephesus (Ancient Greece) in AD 100 at the age of 93. The Gospel of John was likely written by his community more than 60 years after Jesus' crucifixion. In contrast, the other apostles, who traveled to various regions of the world to spread their testimony about Jesus, faced severe persecution, and they likely all died by execution. Their suffering was intense, and it is conceivable that they might have endured much less had they chosen to remain silent and live quiet lives.

The Gospels depict them not as heroes or men of exceptional skill but as ordinary individuals, often with flaws and shortcomings. Jesus' choice of such unlikely individuals for his closest followers reflects a pattern similar to God's selection of figures in the Old Testament. I see no other explanation for their fate than that their experiences with Jesus simplified all their future decisions.

Their faith must have bordered on certainty. This may be difficult to imagine, which is why I recommend reading the story of Joan of Arc—a poor, illiterate teenage peasant girl whom God called to lead the French armies against English occupiers to end the Hundred Years' War. Her story offers valuable insight into the anatomy of the life of an apostle—someone posted by God.

Therefore, instead of detailed contemporary documentation by an independent professional, we have 4 partially independent accounts—the Gospels—each containing testimony for which ordinary individuals of no remarkable virtues went to their deaths without hesitation. While I cannot fully explain why both types of records do not exist, it seems clear which would have been more effective in preserving the message over the centuries if only one were available. Ultimately, as with all matters concerning God, the decision is yours.

To summarize, we have identified Jesus of Nazareth as the one candidate for a man in whom God did not relinquish control of his consciousness. The overwhelming academic consensus affirms that Jesus was a real historical figure. Even those who question his historicity do not dispute that his earliest followers willingly faced death, without hope of worldly rewards, to testify about him to often hostile strangers across various regions. They did so selflessly, out of love. A core part of their testimony was that Jesus was fully human yet absolutely incapable of acting outside of God's will in anything he did.

Now, let's return to the objections regarding pre-existing myths. If his followers had been captivated by myths foretelling someone like Jesus, then what they witnessed in him must have felt like seeing those myths come to life. The poor fishermen of Galilee were certainly not driven to martyrdom by abstract theories (by some contemporary analogs of our software models). Their faith arose from something far more immediate and intimate.

Our situation is vastly different from theirs. What we can conclude for now—ignoring all myths—is that we have identified a real historical figure who, with remarkable certainty, stands out as the true Son of God (as defined in Part One). From our perspective, no other mythical or historical figure meets the criteria we have established. Therefore, it is highly unlikely that the core identity of Jesus of Nazareth was accidentally constructed from secondary elements of pre-existing myths. In my opinion, the opposite direction seems more likely. However, as with all matters concerning God, one can always choose to dismiss everything as mere coincidence.

It is fair to acknowledge that our findings are not new—many have discovered the same long before us. The oldest testimony about Christ Jesus doesn't come from the Gospels. At least a decade earlier, a Jewish-Greek Pharisee named Saul—a highly educated intellectual well-versed in philosophical concepts like logos and biblical study—wrote numerous epistles to the early Christian communities while traveling around the Mediterranean. Nothing we have recognized was absent from Saul's writings, which can be regarded as the first systematic study of God—the first theology. While our terminology may differ, the reasoning is analogous. Saul was another of God's unexpected choices—a Pharisee who ruthlessly persecuted early Christians until he, like Joan of Arc, had a life-changing apparition. From that moment on, he was known by his new name, Paul the Apostle.

There are multiple paths to God, one of which is science—the path we have attempted to follow. However, in our age, that path seems nearly closed. Yet another path remains open—the path of the humanities. Studying human cultures and history reveals countless myths that, in various ways, appear to foreshadow Christ across different times and civilizations. Though I am not deeply versed in the humanities, profoundly learned Catholics like J.R.R. Tolkien have viewed ancient mythology as evidence pointing toward Christ. In fact, Tolkien sought to guide others to Christ through his own 'artificial myths,' woven into his works—most notably, The Lord of the Rings.

His close friend, C.S. Lewis, a professor of ancient literature at Oxford and the author of The Chronicles of Narnia (another example of myth woven into Christian allegory), was also one of the most influential Christian apologists of the twentieth century. His works include Mere Christianity, The Allegory of Love, and The Screwtape Letters. For Lewis, mythical foreshadowing played a key role in rekindling his faith in Jesus, which he had lost in his teenage years.

Below are several myths that some interpret as foreshadowing Christ. Equally well, we could say that Christ turns these myths on their heads:

Osiris (Egyptian Mythology): Osiris is killed, dismembered, and then brought back to life by his wife, Isis. His resurrection symbolizes renewal and immortality.

Tammuz or Dumuzi (Mesopotamian Mythology): The god Tammuz dies annually and descends into the underworld, only to rise again, symbolizing the cycles of death and rebirth tied to the seasons.

Adonis (Greek Mythology): A beloved youth of Aphrodite, he is killed by a wild boar but resurrected by Zeus for part of each year.

Horus (Egyptian Mythology): The son of Osiris and Isis, he is often depicted as a god who takes human form to fight evil, symbolizing the triumph of good over darkness.

Krishna (Hindu Mythology): An avatar (incarnation) of the god Vishnu, he comes to earth to protect the righteous, defeat evil, and establish dharma (moral order). His life includes miracles and a divine mission.

Prometheus (Greek Mythology): A Titan who defies Zeus by giving fire (symbolic of knowledge and life) to humanity. He is severely punished and suffers for this act of sacrificial rebellion. Prometheus is finally freed by the hero Heracles.

Baldr (Norse Mythology): The beloved son of Odin, is a god of light, purity, and goodness. He is prophesied to die, which causes great sorrow in the gods' realm. His death marks the beginning of the events leading to Ragnarok (the end of the world). However, after Ragnarok, Baldr is resurrected and returns to rule in the new world.

Mithras (Roman Mystery Religion): The central figure of the Roman Mithraic mystery cult, he was believed to have been born of a virgin and was associated with the sun, justice, and salvation. Mithraism involved a ritual meal and the belief in Mithras' victory over darkness. Some scholars have noted parallels between Mithraic rituals and Christian sacraments.

Quetzalcoatl (Mesoamerican Mythology): The feathered serpent god of the Aztecs, he is often associated with light, knowledge, and creation. In some versions of the myth, Quetzalcoatl sacrifices himself and promises to return.

I do not believe that knowledge of history and culture alone provides a solid foundation for personal faith. While science continuously refines itself, advancing toward a more precise understanding of logos, historical interpretation remains far more fluid. Historical narratives may be persuasive, but their inherent uncertainty makes them an unreliable foundation for life's most important decisions. I argue that firsthand, intimate experience—*the private baby-like research*—should always take precedence in shaping faith. Daily choices should not depend on someone else's interpretation of history or ancient texts. Faith cannot be delegated to historians, sociologists, cultural theorists, theologians, or other eloquent voices. The pursuit of truth is a deeply personal endeavor, and to outsource it is to compromise your own humanity.

That said, history and culture serve as valuable tools for deepening faith, amplifying our inner voice—the calling of the Holy Spirit. To attune yourself to God's message, there is no better practice than immersing yourself in the Gospels, the writings of St. Paul, the New Testament, and ultimately, the entire Bible. If what you read resonates deeply with your inner voice and personal search for truth, it will provide a certainty as firm as any.

However, if your personal experience and inner voice seem at odds with Scripture, it is essential to explore the historical and cultural context of these ancient texts before dismissing them as not divinely inspired. Rather than focusing on isolated verses, read entire chapters or books of the Bible to grasp the broader message. Study scholars who analyze the original texts to uncover what may have been lost or altered in translation. Explore the lives and historical contexts of early Christian communities and the people of Israel, paying close attention to their symbols, analogies, and references. Remember, every text serves a purpose. The Gospels, for instance, were not written with the expectation that they would be used globally for the next two millennia.

It is crucial to emphasize that, as Catholics, we worship the Lord, not the Bible. If scientific findings appear to contradict Scripture, it's a problem. Joseph Ratzinger addresses this tension by discussing historical science, emphasizing that its strict reliance on documentary and archaeological evidence "not only reveals but also conceals history." However, if there were a historical consensus, for instance, that Jesus was not a real figure, it could not simply be dismissed by blind faith. Doing so would amount to fanaticism, which is contrary to faith.

Fanaticism is a common mechanism of avoiding uncertainty, a kind of religious drug that allows people to feel certain without wrestling with doubts and questions and making peace with them. It's a trap that leads to delusion and, in extreme cases, the worst kinds of actions. Fanaticism—a self-imposed faith—is like being frozen in adolescence forever. You may follow all the commandments to the letter and recite all the correct formulas, but you will likely find yourself breaking those same commandments in profound ways and leading a double life very soon because no one can love God just formally, out of their own will. Love for God is a gift received after one earnestly prepares their heart—as we will explore in the final chapter. Part of being ready is learning to live with humility and admit that you do not, and cannot, fully understand everything all the time.

Lamb of God

The Church teaches that through the sacrifice of Christ, the sins of the world may be forgiven. This belief is foundational to Catholicism and Christianity as a whole. However, to truly embrace this teaching, we must do more than simply accept it at face value. We must strive to understand its meaning as clearly as possible. Without such understanding, how could it have any real impact on our lives? In my view, this is one of those cases where the Church—its mainstream—provides the right answers but fails to present them in an understandable way for believers today.

Let's start with where it all begins. And by all, I mean both the public ministry of Jesus and the Church's discourse on His sacrifice. It is in this Gospel passage that John the Baptist, when questioned by the Pharisees, explains why he baptizes others:

24 Now the Pharisees who had been sent
25   questioned him, "Why then do you baptize
      if you are not the Messiah, nor Elijah, nor the Prophet?"
26   "I baptize with water," John replied,
      "but among you stands one you do not know.
27   He is the one who comes after me,
      the straps of whose sandals I am not worthy to untie."
28   This all happened at Bethany
      on the other side of the Jordan,
      where John was baptizing.
29   The next day John saw Jesus coming toward him
      and said,
      "Look, the Lamb of God,

who takes away the sin of the world!
30   This is the one I meant when I said,
      'A man who comes after me has surpassed me
      because he was before me.'
31   I myself did not know him,
      but the reason I came baptizing with water was
      that he might be revealed to Israel."   **John 1:24–31 (NIV)**

In this passage, John the Baptist describes Jesus, though younger than him in age, as existing before time ("who was before me"). He also likens Jesus to a sacrificial lamb, an animal offered to God to reconcile humanity with Him. This powerful imagery conveys the idea of Jesus as the ultimate sacrifice, bridging the gap between God and humanity created by sin—our shared debt to truth.

To understand John's analogy, it helps to first summarize how the ancient practice of ritual sacrifice worked: Ritual sacrifice was widespread across most ancient cultures, even among those in the Americas, which developed independently. Even before Christ, people acknowledged moral wrongdoing and considered certain actions as sins. Because of their flawed model of God, they feared Him and believed they could appease His wrath by offering something of great value—usually an animal—as a form of penal sacrifice.

They imagined God as a powerful, invisible ruler, independent of their world, rather than as the owner of all things—including their animals and even their very consciousness. Since they had no way to physically offer payment to God, they often burned the sacrificed animals as a publicly visible demonstration of their loss. These animals were seen as substitutes, or proxies, taking the people's sins upon themselves.

A modern observer might wonder why they didn't instead choose to imprison themselves, whip themselves, or fast. While the exact reasoning is uncertain, it's possible that such extreme acts of personal suffering posed too great a risk to their survival and that of their families. Or did they, even then, intuit that tearing down the delusion of righteousness must always come first?

Either way, although they acknowledged God's absolute power, they failed to see Him as the source of love and care in the world. Today, however, we can interpret God this way based on the Old Testament alone. Had they done the same, they might have replaced destructive rituals with acts of love and charity—something many people today—believers and nonbelievers alike—strive to do, influenced by the teachings of Jesus.

Both then and now, magical thinking has influenced human behavior. The widespread belief was that gods, spiritual energies, or supernatural forces could be bribed through esoteric rituals. In their flawed perception of divine reason (Logos), they often viewed God as an all-powerful vending machine—where sacrifices or offerings were exchanged for divine favors. Today, we see a resurgence of these pre-Christian ideas, as increasing numbers of people embrace similar notions of manipulating imagined spiritual forces through rituals and mystical practices.

In summary, people needed to break free from their flawed model of God. Christ Jesus sacrificed Himself out of love, seeking to correct this distorted view of God. In this, He undoubtedly succeeded. Even the Jewish community, after the destruction of the Second Temple in 70 AD, abandoned the practice of animal sacrifice. Instead, Pharisaic teachings shifted the focus toward acts of love and charity, repentance, prayer, and the study of sacred texts—though this transition remains debated within Judaism today.

In this context, Ratzinger cites an insightful observation from Louis Evely. Evely suggests that Christ came to draw humanity to Himself, inviting us to become more like God—a theme explored in the previous chapter. Interestingly, Adam is also depicted in the Bible as one who sought to be like God. He even attempted to blame God for his actions, arguing that it was God who had given him the woman responsible for his downfall. Evely wrote:

> The entire history of humanity was led astray, broken because of Adam's false conception of God. He wanted to become like God. I hope you never saw Adam's sin in this... Did God not invite him to do so? Adam was simply mistaken in his model. He believed that God was an independent, autonomous being, self-sufficient in himself, and in his desire to become like him, he rebelled and showed disobedience.
>
> But when God revealed himself, when he wanted to show who he truly was, he appeared as love, as tenderness, as the outpouring of himself—an infinite delight in another. Affec-

tion, dependence. God revealed himself as obedient, obedient unto death.

In believing he was becoming like God, Adam strayed completely from him. He withdrew into solitude, while God is,
in his very nature, [holy] communion.

As seen in the passage below, the author of the Epistle to the Hebrews
highlights the inefficacy of animal sacrifices and quotes Jesus, who came
to end "the first in order to establish the second". In this context, the
'second' refers to the perfect fulfillment of God's will. In terms of our
software analogy, this fulfillment of God's will means freely and willingly—out of love—surrendering control back to Him in our consciousness. The author also underscores the transition from living under 'the
law' (way of life) to faith in Christ Jesus, marking a shift in how God is
understood. Observe also how Jesus, in His prayer, acknowledges the
body God prepared for His incarnation, knowing that He will endure
physical torture and death at the hands of men:

[1] For since the law has but a shadow
of the good things to come
instead of the true form of these realities,
it can never, by the same sacrifices
that are continually offered every year,
make perfect those who draw near.
[2] Otherwise, would they not have ceased to be offered,
since the worshipers, having once been cleansed,
would no longer have any consciousness of sins?
[3] But in these sacrifices
there is a reminder of sins every year.
[4] **For it is impossible for the blood of bulls and goats
to take away sins.**
[5] Consequently, when Christ came into the world, he said,
"Sacrifices and offerings you have not desired,
but a body have you prepared for me;
[6] in burnt offerings and sin offerings
you have taken no pleasure.
[7] Then I said,
'Behold, I have come to do your will, O God,

as it is written of me in the scroll of the book.'"
8   When he said above,
    "You have neither desired nor taken pleasure
    in sacrifices and offerings and burnt offerings
    and sin offerings"
    (these are offered according to the law),
9   then he added, **"Behold, I have come to do your will."**
    He does away with the first
    in order to establish the second.
10 And by that will we have been sanctified
    through the offering of the body of Jesus Christ
    once for all.   **Hebrews 10:1–10 (ESV)**

We have now reached a point where it should be evident that Christ Jesus came to reshape humanity's model of God. Clearly, after His sacrifice on the cross, no further sacrificial offerings are needed. However, we need to explore how His perfect obedience to God's will took away our sins and which sins, in particular, this refers to. Additionally, we need to explore whether Christ's torture and death were truly required for this transformation.

Before we begin, we turn to Joseph Ratzinger, who critiques a parody of the explanation of these questions—one that still persists in some circles today. This distorted view seeks to return Christianity to a model of God as an all-powerful vending machine, devoid of love and driven by merciless transactions. This perspective fuels the *alternative Christian faith* of certain Christian hardliners today:

As we have already established, the universal Christian consciousness in this matter is extensively influenced by a much-coarsened version of St. Anselm's theology of atonement, the main lines of which we have considered in another context. To many, many Christians, and especially to those who only know the faith from a fair distance, it looks as if the Cross is to be understood as part of a mechanism of injured and restored right. It is the form, so it seems, in which the infinitely offended righteousness of God was propitiated again by means of an infinite expiation. It thus appears to people as the expression of an attitude that insists on a precise balance between debit and credit. At the same time one gets the feeling that this balance is based, nevertheless, on a fiction. One gives first secretly with the left hand what one takes back again ceremonially with the right. The 'infinite expiation' on which God seems to insist thus moves into a doubly sinister light. Many devotional texts actually force one to think that Christian faith in the Cross imagines a God whose unrelenting righteousness demanded a human sacrifice, the sacrifice of his own Son, and one turns away in horror from a righteousness whose sinister wrath makes the message of love incredible.

Let's begin by asking whether Jesus' torture and death were truly necessary. From a purely technical perspective, the answer is: No, it wasn't. Every individual involved in this miscarriage of justice had free will and could have chosen to prevent His execution. We can speculate that if Jesus' ministry alone had been sufficient to reconcile humanity with God, He might have died of natural causes, and God could still have resurrected Him. Unfortunately, it wasn't. His brutal execution was not a divine necessity but a tragically certain consequence of human choices.

Whenever human choice is involved, God never acts as though the outcome is predetermined. He continually offers redemption, even when He knows it will not be accepted—just as the laws of physics remain unchanged, whether or not they seem to matter. Without this consistency, we could not learn or comprehend them.

Now, let's examine the events leading up to Jesus' arrest in the Garden of Gethsemane:

38 Then he told them,
   "I'm so deeply grieved that I feel I'm about to die.
   Wait here and stay awake with me."
39   Going on a little farther, he fell on his face and prayed,
   "O my Father, if it is possible, let this cup pass from me.
   Yet not what I want but what you want."
40   When he went back to the disciples,
   he found them asleep.
   He told Peter, "So, you men couldn't stay awake
   with me for one hour, could you?"   **Matthew 26:38–40 (ISV)**

In various parts of his book, Ratzinger explores the profound mystery of Jesus—who is consubstantial with the Father—yet speaks to Him as a distinct person. Was Jesus' cry from the cross—"Father, forgive them, for they know not what they do"—merely a theatrical gesture? I don't believe so. We must remember that God the Father observed Jesus in the Garden of Gethsemane and also beheld His suffering on the cross. He saw through the eyes of both His apostles and His persecutors. And now, He watches through us, the readers of this very text. To this Father, Jesus pleaded; to this Father, He showed compassion as He endured abandonment and crucifixion. Thus, God the Father is distinct from the Lord Jesus, yet inseparably united with Him.

Just before His death, Jesus cried out the words of Psalm 22: "Eli, Eli, lema sabachthani?" These words, preserved in Aramaic—Jesus' native tongue—are likely His very own. They mean, "My God, my God, why have you forsaken me?"

Throughout His life, Jesus consistently addressed the Father as 'Abba' (meaning 'Daddy') rather than 'Eli' (which means 'personal God'). Notably, He never repeated the word 'Abba' in succession, as one might do when reciting verses of a song. Each of us must decide whether these words express doubt or serve as a profound reference to Psalm 22—a passage so strikingly descriptive that it seems written for this very moment in history. If these words conveyed doubt and separation, it would contradict our software analogy, as Jesus could not be estranged from Himself.

The crucifixion was not merely an act of violence—it was the ultimate rejection of God's love, a betrayal of the One who became man to reveal His true image. Jesus knew what was about to happen. Though it was not His desire to suffer, He understood that this singular event—the gravest act of human rejection toward God—would deeply shake many. Jesus knew that once we sobered up and realized the gravity of what we had done, many would turn away in horror from what we all have become since the fall of Adam. He knew that, in that moment of reckoning, many would recognize the need to abandon the old way of life in favor of the ultimate love God revealed to us on the cross. Jesus gifted us the ultimate instance of turning the other cheek, hoping it would lead us to finally say No to evil through baptism.

This is how the baptism ceremony proceeds:

Priest: Do you reject sin
so as to live in the freedom of God's children?
Catechumen: I do.

Priest: Do you reject the glamour of evil,
and refuse to be mastered by sin?
Catechumen: I do.

Priest: Do you reject Satan,
father of sin, and prince of darkness?
Catechumen: I do.

Priest: Do you believe in God, the Father almighty,
creator of heaven and earth?
Catechumen: I do believe.

Priest: Do you believe in Jesus Christ,
his only Son, our Lord,
who was born of the Virgin Mary,
was crucified, died, and was buried,
rose from the dead,
and is now seated at the right hand of the Father?
Catechumen: I do believe.

Priest: Do you believe in the Holy Spirit,
the holy Catholic Church, the communion of saints,
the forgiveness of sins, the resurrection of the body,
and the life everlasting?
Catechumen: I do believe.

Priest: I baptize you in the name of the Father,
and of the Son, and of the Holy Spirit.

This is why Jesus sacrificed Himself and died so that many might renounce sin and turn to Him.

[44] It was now about noon, and darkness came
over the whole land until three in the afternoon,
for the sun stopped shining (...).   **Luke 23:44–45 (NIV)**

⁵¹ At that moment the curtain of the temple
was torn in two from top to bottom.
The earth shook, the rocks split.   **Matthew 27:51 (NIV)**

This is how a single man on the cross has shaken all of humanity, causing many to renounce sin and turn to Him through baptism. It is not something that happened once and it is dome. It is a powerful wave set in motion by Christ, one that continues to ripple through history today.

When we return control of our consciousness to God, we become instruments of unconditional love and care ('charitas', 'grace'). Love that knows no debt or credit, no favor or reward. Love that is born purely out of admiration for who God is and what He stands for. Love that no longer has any private 'I' and makes you one with God. With God, who has shown us His complete investment in the world—so much so that it is impossible for Him to be more invested.

As Joseph Ratzinger brilliantly summarizes:

> Whoever puts himself at God's disposal disappears with him in the cloud, into oblivion and insignificance, and precisely in this way acquires a share in his glory.

— 18 —

Heaven or Hell?

At the close of the previous chapter, I quoted a passage from the sacrament of baptism, where one renounces evil and professes faith in the Triune God. In fact, the Creed gradually evolved from these baptismal vows, becoming the central prayer that encapsulates the core tenets of the Catholic faith. We have not yet explored all of the Creed's components, such as Christ's resurrection, eternal life, or the communion of saints. These elements are deeply interconnected; let us discuss them now, starting with the resurrection of Christ.

If the consciousness of God is primordial to this world, it could not have simply ceased to exist when Christ died on the cross. It surely continued after the death of Jesus. On the other hand, this doesn't necessarily imply that Jesus had to appear to people after His resurrection. There must have been a reason for that.

Seemingly, we now speak of miracles as if they were ordinary events. Yet, if God governs the world with the same mastery that a software designer exercises over a virtual simulation, the miracles recorded in the New Testament appear relatively modest—certainly not so overwhelming as to make the world unintelligible—for example, by making rivers flow in the opposite direction. The miracles of Jesus take on far greater significance when viewed through the lens of God's love for man. Thus, instead of asking, "How is that possible?" we should focus on, "What was the purpose?"

For instance, why was it necessary for Jesus to be born of a virgin? One would not need to overturn the entire field of human biology just to achieve a single instance of rare human parthenogenesis (I'm not implying the particular mechanism here, just assessing the feasibility). The real question is: What was the purpose of the virgin birth? Could God have intended to make Jesus' family unsuitable for the creation of a political dynasty? Did Judas Iscariot and the chief priests ultimately betray Jesus because they lost all hope that He would be a warrior worth the House of David? The Messiah they expected to fight the Roman Empire with the sword? We may never know.

While we may never fully grasp the breadth of the purpose of miracles, we can catch glimpses of their possible symbolism and visible consequences. As we explore their purpose and meaning, we gradually enter a realm where we increasingly rely on the word of God. Not because current scientific understanding prevents us from believing that these miracles truly happened, but because to truly comprehend them, we must depend on the testimony of the New Testament. In doing so, we trust that this testimony is accurate enough to guide us in our sincere efforts to understand. This is no small matter—I have found it more challenging to internalize this belief than to merely accept that the miracles occurred. Fortunately, we are also guided by our inner voice—the call of the Holy Spirit—to help us navigate this struggle.

This is how St. Paul summarizes his thoughts on Christ's resurrection in his first epistle to the Corinthians (part of the New Testament of the Bible):

> ³For I passed on to you
> the most important points that I received:
> The Messiah died for our sins
> according to the Scriptures,
> ⁴ he was buried, he was raised on the third day
> according to the Scriptures—and is still alive!
> ⁵ And he was seen by Cephas,
> and then by the Twelve.
> ⁶ After that, he was seen by more than 500 brothers
> at one time,
> most of whom are still alive,
> though some have died.
> ⁷ Next he was seen by James,
> then by all the apostles,
> ⁸ and finally he was seen by me,
> as though I were born abnormally late.

⁹   For I am the least of the apostles
    and not even fit to be called an apostle
    because I persecuted God's church.

                              1 Corinthians 15:3–9 (ISV)

¹²Now if we preach
    that the Messiah has been raised from the dead,
    how can some of you keep claiming
    there is no resurrection of the dead?
¹³   If there is no resurrection of the dead,
    then the Messiah has not been raised,
¹⁴   and if the Messiah has not been raised,
    then our message means nothing
    and your faith means nothing.
¹⁵   In addition, we are found to be false witnesses about God
    because we testified on God's behalf
    that he raised the Messiah—whom he did not raise
    if in fact it is true that the dead are not raised.
¹⁶   For if the dead are not raised,
    then the Messiah has not been raised,
¹⁷   and if the Messiah has not been raised,
    your faith is worthless
    and you are still imprisoned by your sins.
¹⁸   Yes, even those who have died
    believing in the Messiah are lost.
¹⁹   If we have set our hopes on the Messiah in this life only,
    we deserve more pity than any other people.

                              1 Corinthians 15:12–19 (ISV)

First, it is important to note that when St. Paul refers to the Scriptures, he is referring to the Old Testament, where the life, death, and resurrection of Christ are foretold with remarkable detail. At the time of his writing, the New Testament had not yet been compiled, so he could not refer to it.

Before Christ, there was no clear consensus among Jews regarding eternal life. Some interpreted the Scriptures one way, while others interpreted them differently. St. Paul argues that without Christ's resurrection, there would be neither evidence nor hope that He was the true

Messiah. Without it, Christ would be regarded merely as a wise teacher of divine love—someone we might admire—but admiration alone would leave us as little more than naive idealists. However, if we believe in the reality of Christ's resurrection—as Paul describes it—not only does it serve as evidence that one man has already risen from the dead, but it also reinforces the promise of eternal life that Jesus Himself preached numerous times:

[24]Very truly I tell you, whoever hears my word
and believes him who sent me has eternal life
and will not be judged
but has crossed over from death to life.   **John 5:24 (NIV)**

[16]For God so loved the world
that he gave his one and only Son,
that whoever believes in him
shall not perish
but have eternal life.   **John 3:16 (NIV)**

[28]I give them eternal life, and they shall never perish;
no one will snatch them out of my hand.   **John 10:28 (NIV)**

[40]For my Father's will is
that everyone who looks to the Son and believes in him
shall have eternal life,
and I will raise them up at the last day.   **John 6:40 (NIV)**

[21]"Lord," Martha said to Jesus,
"if you had been here, my brother would not have died.
[22] But I know that even now God will give you
whatever you ask."
[23] Jesus said to her, "Your brother will rise again."
[24] Martha answered, "I know he will rise again
in the resurrection at the last day."
[25] Jesus said to her, "I am the resurrection and the life.
The one who believes in me will live,
even though they die;
[26] and whoever lives by believing in me will never die.
Do you believe this?"   **John 11:21–26 (NIV)**

29 "Truly I tell you," Jesus said to them,
   "no one who has left home or wife or brothers
   or sisters or parents or children
   for the sake of the kingdom of God
30   will fail to receive many times as much in this age,
   and in the age to come eternal life."   **Luke 18:29–30 (NIV)**

16 Just then a man [the wealthy one we already talked about]
   came up to Jesus and asked,
   "Teacher, what good thing must I do to get eternal life?"
17   "Why do you ask me about what is good?" Jesus replied.
   "There is only One who is good.
   If you want to enter life, keep the commandments."
                                    Matthew 19:16–17 (NIV)

We can speculate that St. Paul struggled to explain how Jesus' resurrection implies the resurrection of ordinary people. At the time of his writing, the debate over Jesus being both fully man and fully God had not yet been definitively settled. If Jesus were a fundamentally different kind of being than the rest of humanity, what was true of Him might not necessarily apply to the rest of us. However, if Jesus truly rose from the dead, this event lends significant credibility to His teachings on resurrection and eternal life.

In our software analogy, Jesus is not a fundamentally different 'type' of being but rather an extraordinary example of humanity—an 'edge case.' He is the ideal man—someone without a private 'I,' the ultimate model of what humans can aspire to become. St. Paul even refers to Jesus as the 'ultimate man' in a later part of his first letter to the Corinthians—often translated as the 'last Adam'.

So, in that sense, Jesus was like us. That said, it is beyond doubt that within God's consciousness, countless events unfold—completely estranged from us—of which we know nothing. For instance, we cannot fathom how or when God—step by step—transforms all the randomness we observe in matter into a coherent, meaningful purpose for everyone. Similarly, we know nothing about what transpired in God's consciousness following Jesus' death—except for what the New Testament testifies occurred and was relayed through Him after His resurrection.

This also means the question of what happens in our consciousness after death remains a pressing one. If God has given us our identity and individuality by granting us free will within His own consciousness, could He simply forget us and move on—an idea that aligns with how nonbelievers might perceive death—as a form of final erasure? In a virtual simulation, such a view would be analogous to discarding an entity. In real life, if we compare God's creation of an individual to someone taking control of your own body, the 'destruction' of that individual could be likened to God reclaiming control and erasing all memory of their existence.

While we can imagine what it might feel like to regain control over a free-willed character in a virtual simulation and conceive that God could do something similar in the real world, the idea that He could 'forget an individual' seems highly counterintuitive. Not because His power would be limited, but because the notion of God *experiencing amnesia* may be meaningless. It may be similar to the paradoxical question: "Can an omnipotent God create a stone He cannot lift?"

While the phrase "God experienced amnesia" may be grammatically correct, it could just as easily be a sequence of words devoid of meaning. In the realm of natural language, we can string together many such statements, and we can even use logic to make formally correct inferences on their basis, just as many philosophers do. By contrast, writing code doesn't allow you such nonsense. If you tried to code a world with an 'unliftable stone' in it, you would quickly see the problem. You could define stones as liftable and then label some as unliftable. However, as the system's creator, you would still have the power to lift them, rendering 'unliftable' merely a flawed naming convention within your design. Alternatively, you could redefine 'stone' as something entirely unlike what we know in the physical world. However, this would still result in a flawed representation, failing to reflect the essence of this world—the 'in-itselfness' of stones, which are liftable.

In my view, the idea of God experiencing amnesia—forgetting His own child—is merciless and unworthy of the loving parent God appears to be. From the technical perspective, such a notion appears just as flawed and nonsensical as designing a world devoid of suffering, except for that which we cause ourselves (as we discussed earlier in connection with the Book of Job). Our existence leaves a certain—however subtle—footprint on the universe, and it would turn the world into a designer's nightmare if these traces were routinely backtracked and erased, leaving perhaps only their imprints in matter.

Ratzinger describes a similar opinion as follows:

> The cosmos is not merely an external framework for human history, nor a static structure—a kind of container in which various living beings exist, beings that could just as well be transferred to another container. This means, positively, that the cosmos is movement; that history does not merely take place within it, but that the cosmos itself is history. It is not just the stage on which human history unfolds, even before human history and alongside it—the cosmos itself is history.
>
> Ultimately, there is only one all-encompassing world history, which, despite all its ups and downs, all its advances and re-gressions, still has an overall direction and moves 'forward'.

I find it reasonable to believe that the complete record of our ex-istence resides in God's mind forever, not just its material component. However, this is merely an opinion, and we cannot extrapolate our soft-ware model to explain such metaphysical concepts. In fact, I never in-tentionally stretch the software analogy in this way. The purpose of this book is entirely different: It follows the approach every software engi-neer is trained in—analyzing system's components and constructing a model to integrate them. My goal was to take the content of Introduc-tion to Christianity by Joseph Ratzinger and develop a model that nat-urally accommodates and integrates all its teachings. This model aims to faithfully capture the book's essence (its 'in-itselfness') in a way that coherently unifies all its elements. Just as concepts like atom or pho-ton help explain the physical world in their respective fields, this model seeks to do the same for Catholic teachings about the Triune God. It functions much like a 'modern-day parable,' as do scientific models. Let me emphasize again: The world is not made of *photons*, *atoms*, or *soft-ware analogies*. These are simply conceptual models we use to make sense of reality.

Now, let us return to our reflections on death. While it may seem unreasonable to believe that God would discard any information—and it is worth noting that no software system would either, were it not bound by the constraints of the physical world—it's also clear that God does not grant us access to the entirety of His consciousness at all times. In this sense, He is the master of our experience of time. This is evident from the existence of other beings—other people whom we believe to have consciousness, just as we do, rather than being mere biological machines. Since we do not live their lives, it follows that God must govern our individual experiences of time, granting us moments to 'live,' much like a processor allocates computing time to active processes while others remain suspended.

In this way, it is conceivable that God could temporarily 'pause' our existence. However, if death were merely a 'suspension,' it would imply that death does not truly exist at all. The reason is that even if it took ages for our consciousness to resume—'get some more processing time'—the interval would always seem unnoticeably small from our perspective. Moreover, from our own lived experience, it is impossible to conceive of our consciousness simply ceasing to exist. Most importantly, as we read in the Gospels, Jesus repeatedly promises that it will not. Ultimately, it is up to each of us to decide what we find reasonable to believe among the plausible options.

First, let us quote the official Church teaching from the Compendium of the Catechism of the Catholic Church (CCC), promulgated by Pope Benedict XVI in 2005:

CCC Article 209: By 'heaven' is meant the state of supreme and definitive happiness. Those who die in the grace of God and have no need of further purification are gathered around Jesus and Mary, the angels and the saints. They thus form the Church of heaven, where they see God 'face to face' (1 Corinthians 13:12). They live in a communion of love with the Most Blessed Trinity and they intercede for us.

CCC Article 212: Hell consists in the eternal damnation of those who die in mortal sin through their own free choice. The principal suffering of hell is eternal separation from God in whom alone we can have the life and happiness for which we were created and for which we long. Christ proclaimed this reality with the words, "Depart from me, you cursed, into the eternal fire" (Matthew 25:41 ESV).

In his book, Joseph Ratzinger provides an insightful characterization of the teachings on heaven and hell:

> The Ascension of Christ [to heaven], in turn, points to the other end [than hell] of human existence (an existence infinitely stretched beyond itself, both upward and downward). As the counterpoint to radical isolation, to the untouchability of rejected love, this existence carries within itself the possibility of communion with all other human beings through the encounter with divine love, so that humanity, as it were, can find its geometric place within the very being of God.

> However, the two possibilities of human existence, which are revealed in the words 'heaven' and 'hell', are of entirely different kinds, representing fundamentally distinct ways in which human potential unfolds. The depth we call hell is something that only a person can bring upon themselves. In fact, we must express it even more sharply: Hell consists precisely in the refusal to receive, in the desire for complete self-sufficiency and autonomy. It is the expression of a withdrawal into the purely self-contained. The essence of this depth lies in the refusal to accept, in the unwillingness to receive anything, in the determination to stand entirely on one's own and be self-sufficient. When this attitude reaches its ultimate radicality, the person becomes utterly untouchable, utterly alone, utterly forsaken. Hell is the desire to be only for oneself, the state that arises when a person locks themselves away within their own existence.

> Conversely, the essence of that above—'heaven'—is that it can only be received, just as hell can only be self-imposed. Heaven, by its very nature, is not something self-made or self-achievable. In the language of classical theology, it was said to be a 'donum indebitum et superadditum naturae'—an unmerited gift bestowed upon nature. Heaven can only ever be given to a person as the fulfillment of love, whereas their hell is the loneliness of the one who refuses to accept it, who rejects the status of a beggar and withdraws into themselves.

If, after death, we are to encounter God "face to face," and considering Joseph Ratzinger's points that heaven can "only be received," and hell "can only be self-imposed," the most fitting analogy in our software framework might involve something of a reversal of roles between God and the individual. In such a scenario, God again assumes control of our consciousness—of what we experience—while we recede to become God's inner voices, interceding for the living and the dead.

If, during life, we managed to align ourselves with God—albeit imperfectly—this encounter may be experienced as the perfection of that alignment. If we spent our lives striving to become instruments of love, then Love itself now completes our transformation, granting us an abundance beyond anything we could have ever hoped for. As the previous version of the Catechism states, we reach "the ultimate end and fulfillment of the deepest human longings: The state of supreme, definitive happiness."

The beauty of this configuration lies in the fact that, with God in control of our experience, no barrier remains to prevent us—individuals—from joining a greater communion of interceding inner voices within one common consciousness—the 'Communion of Saints' in Catholic terms. It is also hardly surprising that even after death, we continue to have a purpose: Intercession. I speculate that without purpose, we could hardly experience the profound happiness of sharing in divine love. Either way, as Catholics, we pray to the saints, seeking their intercession on our behalf—implying that they must have some awareness of the world of the living.

While no one knows exactly what transpires in heaven, I suspect it involves transforming the randomness of the material world into a coherent, meaningful purpose for the living—step by step—perhaps even reaching "500 distinct people at one time." If we can truly pray to saints, it follows that heaven is not a separate, isolated, and more perfect *second world* but rather a dimension of the single, unified world we all inhabit.

[9] But as it is written,
"No eye has seen,
no ear has heard,
and no mind has imagined
the things that God has prepared
for those who love him." **1 Corinthians 2:9 (ISV)**

On the other hand, for someone who has rejected God—who did not long to become an instrument of love but instead became entrenched in nurturing their private 'I' or the collective 'We' of societal sins—the exact same experience of God assuming control might feel profoundly different. To such a person, this may be perceived as a total loss of free will—an existence imposed upon them, one they dread and resist. They may feel that even more than what they possessed in their earthly lives has now been taken from them. With their merciless, hardliner hearts hardened against love, these individuals may barricade themselves within, desperately clinging to their individuality in a state of complete isolation, unwilling to accept the love and unity that heaven offers.

Jesus summarizes the transition to abundance in heaven or losing everything in hell as follows:

10 The disciples came to him and asked,
       "Why do you speak to the people in parables?"
11   He replied, "Because the knowledge of the secrets
       of the kingdom of heaven has been given to you,
       but not to them.
12   Whoever has will be given more,
       and they will have an abundance.
       Whoever does not have,
       even what they have will be taken from them."
13   "This is why I speak to them in parables:
       'Though seeing, they do not see;
       though hearing, they do not hear or understand.'
14   In them is fulfilled the prophecy of Isaiah:
       'You will be ever hearing but never understanding;
       you will be ever seeing but never perceiving.
15   For this people's heart has become calloused;
       they hardly hear with their ears,
       and they have closed their eyes.
       Otherwise they might see with their eyes,
       hear with their ears,
       understand with their hearts and turn,
       and I would heal them.'"   **Matthew 13:10–15 (NIV)**

According to Catholic teaching on purgatory, there is also a third possibility: A state in which a person undergoes purification and suffering until they are fully reconciled with their new form of existence. This process ultimately prepares them and transitions them into the fullness of heaven:

> **CCC Article 210:** Purgatory is the state of those who die in God's friendship, assured of their eternal salvation, but who still have need of purification to enter into the happiness of heaven.

I pray that the wealthy young men of this world, who adhere to the 'way of life' yet are unwilling to become instruments of love and follow Jesus, will ultimately find their way to heaven. However, from a human perspective, this seems unlikely, as heaven is the antithesis of a transactional view of salvation. Yet, as Jesus said, "With God all things are possible."

Indeed, it doesn't make much sense to view entry into Heaven as a reward for accumulating a high score of good deeds. First, it's not merely about performing random acts of kindness, but about following God's will and doing the good He desires in each situation. Second, what matters is not the score, not even the correct understanding and full acceptance of faith's doctrine, but rather the state of your soul at the moment of death. Of course, the state of your soul is shaped by concrete actions—just as becoming an excellent organ player requires frequent practice, not merely pressing keys often or simply appreciating organ music.

For those who perceive Jesus as a more lenient version of the 'God of the Old Testament,' I hope it becomes clear that the 'God of the New Testament' desires more than mere adherence to commandments and burnt sacrifices.

As Joseph Ratzinger puts it:

> Letting God act upon us—that is the Christian sacrifice.

And as the New Testament reads:

²⁴Then Jesus said to his disciples,
    "Whoever wants to be my disciple must deny themselves
    and take up their cross and follow me.
²⁵ For whoever wants to save their life will lose it,
    but whoever loses their life for me will find it.
²⁶ What good will it be for someone
    to gain the whole world,
    yet forfeit their soul?
    Or what can anyone give in exchange for their soul?"
Matthew 16:24–26 (NIV)

One of the last components of the Creed that we have yet to discuss in this chapter states: "Christ descended into hell."

As Joseph Ratzinger explains, 'hell' in this context is not meant to be understood literally, but rather as a reference to the general experience of death. Before Christ, the Bible used a single term to describe both 'death' and 'hell'—a significant detail, as we will soon see:

Ratzinger writes:

> Let us first take note of an exegetical clarification. We are told that in our article of faith, the word 'hell' is merely a mistranslation of 'Sheol' (Greek: Hades), which, for the Hebrew mind, referred to the state beyond death—vaguely conceived as a kind of shadowy existence, more non-being than being.

Let's also quote the New Testament:

¹⁸For Christ also suffered once for sins,
    the righteous for the unrighteous,
    to bring you to God.
    He was put to death in the body
    but made alive in the Spirit.
¹⁹ After being made alive, he went
    and made proclamation to the imprisoned spirits.
1 Peter 3:18–19 (NIV)

¹Therefore, since Christ suffered in his body,
   arm yourselves also with the same attitude,
   because whoever suffers in the body is done with sin.
2   As a result, they do not live the rest of their earthly lives
   for evil human desires, but rather for the will of God.
3   For you have spent enough time in the past
   doing what pagans choose to do—living in
   debauchery, lust, drunkenness,
   orgies, carousing and detestable idolatry.
4   They are surprised that you do not join them
   in their reckless, wild living,
   and they heap abuse on you.
5   But they will have to give account to him
   who is ready to judge the living and the dead.
6   **For this is the reason the gospel was preached**
   even to those who are now dead,
   so that they might be judged
   according to human standards in regard to the body,
   but live according to God in regard to the spirit.
                                    1 Peter 4:1–6 (NIV)

It is evident that this testimony applies to all people after death—both the righteous and the unrighteous. Within our software analogy, this suggests that everyone, regardless of their alignment with or rejection of God, will encounter His direct presence after death. Their consciousness will neither be erased nor indefinitely suspended 'in the state of Sheol.' This provides a measure of hope for those who did not die in perfect alignment with God. However, it also foretells suffering for those who have irrevocably chosen to reject Him.

Certain passages of the New Testament suggest that some of these "imprisoned spirits" may have existed in a suspended state of consciousness—a shadowy existence of 'Sheol,' more nonbeing than being—for a very long time until Christ came and the Gospel was preached to them (whatever this metaphor entails). Only then did the heavenly reality become possible.

Although we may never fully grasp the specifics, the underlying message about *breaking the gates* of that provisional state of suspension (Sheol) remains clear, as expressed in this biblical quote:

[18] And I tell you that you are Peter, and on this rock I will build my church, and the gates of Hades [Sheol, Hell] will not overcome it.   **Matthew 16:18 (NIV)**

— 19 —

The End

There is one dimension of faith we haven't yet addressed in this book, and in many ways, it is the most essential: Reverence. If we genuinely love God and strive to submit to His will, allowing His love—not ire, not justice, not truth, but love—to act through us, it would be difficult to keep this faith contained within ourselves. We are not isolated islands, meant to keep faith hidden in private realms. Yet we also can't step into public spaces and improvise acts of worship based purely on our momentary whim.

If you feel now, reading this, that it is your sovereign human right to worship God in any way you choose, legally speaking, you are correct—at least if you live in the free world. However, it also means your private 'I' still blocks the view. I remember the first time I entered a church. I did so, filled with a deep fear that my ignorance of proper worship might somehow desecrate the Holy Mass. You can study the form, but that's about it. Reason can guide you up to this point in the book, but faith in Him transcends reason—it encompasses the heart. And perhaps faith is more of the heart than of reason in the end.

Reason can prepare you to freely and willingly say Yes to God, but such faith alone cannot save you, for it does not set your heart on fire. Only God can do that, and He offers it as a gift when you are ready to accept it. Love for God is like the nominal faith set on fire. However, once that fire is kindled within your heart, you cannot treat it carelessly. There must be a reverent way to nurture and express this love—one that reflects the deep devotion and respect God is due in your eyes. Reverent worship cannot be arbitrary—arbitrary worship lacks reverence by definition. This means our worship needs to be orderly, and an orderly worship is called liturgy.

Liturgy is not something that can be crafted by reason alone. If it were simply our own creation, how could we trust it to be independent and objective? Designing your own liturgy is like trying to save yourself from drowning by pulling up on your own hair. It's as pointless as seeking to give your life a purpose without adding God into the conversation.

All the liturgy of the Catholic Church originates from the Lord Jesus Himself. And this is also part of the reason why the Creed refers to it as "the holy, catholic, and apostolic Church." It is not holy because of us—the sinners who make up the Church—nor because of the flawed human institutions that govern it. The Church is holy because its foundation and its liturgy come from God Himself and because the Holy Spirit dwells in it. The Bible uses the term 'in Christ'—we are cells of the imperfect collective body of Christ, who is holy.

If we see the Church as a living organism, then the liturgy functions as one of its vital organs. It evolves over time, with reason playing a key role in this evolution. However, it is essential to recognize that the liturgy is not something we create for ourselves; rather, it is a gift from Him who breathed life into the body of the Church.

For those devoted to God, prioritizing Him above all else, it is essential to worship properly and with reverence. This includes properly and reverently joining the body of the Church, growing and maturing there, being nourished, living, being healed, as well as facing illness and death. Additionally, for the Church, it is vital to uphold the content of the faith properly: At the liturgical level, within the local community, and through as perfect reflection of the logos of faith as possible.

To bring these aspects of the Church's life to fulfillment, we were given the sacraments and their corresponding liturgies. We enter the Church through the sacrament of Baptism, where we renounce evil and say Yes to the Triune God. The sacrament of Penance offers reconciliation with God when we stray. Confirmation matures us in our faith. The sacrament of Marriage helps us live in grace within our most intimate community—the family. The Anointing of the Sick provides comfort as we face illness and death. Above all, the Eucharist sustains us spiritually, which means it helps us maintain proper reverence for the Lord Jesus.

Additionally, the three degrees of the sacrament of Holy Orders—deacon, priest, and bishop—are essential for ministering to the faith community. The Church is called 'apostolic' due to the uninterrupted line of succession of faith ministers beginning with the Lord Jesus.

According to the Compendium of the Catechism of the Catholic Church (CCC) promulgated by the Pope in 2005 AD:

> **CCC 224:** The sacraments, instituted by Christ and entrusted to the Church, are efficacious signs of grace perceptible to the senses. Through them divine life is bestowed upon us (...).

While it is possible to live without sacraments and still align ourselves with God—becoming instruments of Love—there is a clear, tangible difference between living in God's grace and merely longing for it. Sacraments are not empty customs, traditions, or symbols invented by human means. For example, if you love God but are not baptized, you naturally long for baptism, and your inner experience differs from that of a baptized Christian who actively receives God's grace and is properly aligned with Him. I have never encountered anyone who understands the faith as described in this book, loves God deeply from the heart rather than just intellectually, and yet willingly avoids the sacraments without some objective obstacle in the way.

Of course, not everyone is called to receive every sacrament. Not all are called to marriage, for instance. Different types of vows exist within various communities. For diocesan priests, the parish becomes their family, and they serve as spiritual fathers to their congregants. Other communities can also become family in a sense. Spiritual orders, for instance, may have their own vows. While not sacraments, these vows reflect a similar desire to live in God's grace with proper reverence.

At their core, all people naturally desire to attain a sacramental level of grace and certainty in their lives—not just Catholics, Christians, or believers. Even devout atheists feel this attraction, despite the fact that, in theory, they should not—if they had fully internalized their rejection of faith. A clear example is the institution of civil marriage or the ongoing struggle for what is now commonly referred to as 'universal marriage rights.' More broadly, this unconscious drive is evident in the fight for human rights, which seeks to affirm the inherent dignity of all human beings through legal means.

In my view, humanity feels an increasing attraction—whether conscious or unconscious—to living sacramentally: In God's grace, in inner peace, and in reverence for the Lord Jesus, who draws all to Himself. At times, this attraction feels as undeniable as the forces of nature. Yet often, the effort fails—much like trying to save oneself from drowning by pulling up on one's own hair. Therefore, from an engineer's perspective, I confidently assert that the scenario in which the whole planet ultimately starts converting to Catholicism is by far the most likely. It resembles a vortex in a sink. While those trained in the humanities might celebrate the elegance of diverse worldview streams, practical engineers like me see the inevitable convergence of this intricate system.

Before moving on from sacramentality, let's reflect on the Eucharist (literally meaning 'thanksgiving'), which plays a central role in nurturing our reverence for the Lord Jesus.

Earlier in this book, I noted that God set apart the final day as sacred, thereby establishing the very concept of sacredness. Something sacred is set apart and treated differently. There is no physical difference that makes something sacred; rather, it is our attitude toward that thing that fosters reverence within us. For Christians, sacred things exist to serve us, not to be served.

From a scientific perspective, Sunday is no different from any other day. The increased number of Catholic Masses held worldwide on Sundays has no material effect on the planet. However, on an internal, spiritual level, proper reverence would be impossible without a real presence of the sacred—a sacred time, in the case of Sunday.

Similarly, without the real presence of the sacred, a church becomes nothing more than a meeting room. For meeting rooms, it is absolutely inappropriate to be heavily decorated in the manner that Catholic churches are. Such lavishness would constitute kitsch worthy of an oriental Marxist oligarch. To such a person, it may fit since—as we have discussed—he holds the position of false God.

Sadly, it's easy to misplace our sense of what is truly sacred. Before Christ, people often revered sacred wells, trees, and sculptures—an inclination that led to idolatry, polytheism, and magic, as we've discussed earlier. An improper understanding of the sacred can lead to confusion, which underscores the Eucharist's role in helping us direct our reverence properly toward God.

Let's now experience the Eucharist through the eyes of a *little baby-like researcher*:

When you enter Protestant churches, mosques, or synagogues, the atmosphere feels different. But stepping into a Catholic church, there is an undeniable sense of the sacred inside. Also, in Catholic churches, while some believers attend liturgies during the week, everyone always gathers for the Holy Mass every Sunday, a day set apart as sacred to celebrate the thanksgiving of the Eucharist.

At the beginning of the Mass, everyone examines their conscience as if to avoid the delusion of righteousness, as though preparing to approach God without provoking his righteous anger. The Mass culminates in the celebration of the Last Supper, where the priest, acting in the person of Christ, guides the congregation as they consciously participate in a shared, sacred reality. As the priest repeats the words of the Lord Jesus during the Last Supper, he handles the bread and wine with the utmost reverence that sacred things deserve.

He says:

Take this, all of you, and eat of it,
for this is my body,
which will be given up for you.

In a similar way, when supper was ended,
he took this precious chalice
in his holy and venerable hands,
and once more giving thanks,
he said the blessing
and gave the chalice to his disciples, saying:

Take this, all of you, and drink from it,
for this is the chalice of my blood,
the blood of the new and eternal covenant,
which will be poured out for you and for many
for the forgiveness of sins.
Do this in memory of me.

The people now approach the priest, receiving the bread and wine with profound reverence, united as one community. This sacred act is called Holy Communion, emphasizing the unity of the faithful as they partake in the Body and Blood of Christ. It evokes His sacrifice, through which God revealed Himself as the ultimate source of unconditional love for all ages. This is not merely a distant memory; it continues here and now through His mystical body—the Church—in the lives of the faithful, who strive to sacrifice their private 'I' to become instruments of Love.

Now, when you reflect on this, doesn't it closely resemble how we previously described heaven? God is in control. Everyone first undergoes purification and then whispers their thanks. A united community, sharing one sacred reality—offering thanks, receiving His gifts, and remembering His ultimate act of self-emptying love on the cross. Even prayers of intercession—for both the living and the dead—are woven into every Holy Mass.

It is worth noting that many are absent from the church—likely preoccupied with things that would be impossible in heaven.

To summarize this observation from the perspective of a little baby-like researcher: Everything points to the reality that the bread and wine truly become the sacred Body and Blood of Christ, though they retain the appearance of bread and wine. It is evident that the faithful believe this, but more importantly, Jesus Himself affirms it in Scripture. He explains it repeatedly, and His audience clearly understands what He means:

48 "I am the bread of life.
49   Your ancestors ate the manna in the wilderness,
        yet they died.
50   But here is the bread that comes down from heaven,
        which anyone may eat and not die.
51   I am the living bread that came down from heaven.
        Whoever eats this bread will live forever.
        This bread is my flesh,
        which I will give for the life of the world."
52   Then the Jews began to argue sharply among themselves,
        "How can this man give us his flesh to eat?"
53   Jesus said to them, "Very truly I tell you,
        unless you eat the flesh of the Son of Man
        and drink his blood, you have no life in you.
54   Whoever eats my flesh and drinks my blood
        has eternal life, and I will raise them up at the last day.
55   For my flesh is real food and my blood is real drink.
56   Whoever eats my flesh and drinks my blood
        remains in me, and I in them.

⁵⁷ Just as the living Father sent me
and I live because of the Father,
so the one who feeds on me will live because of me.
⁵⁸ This is the bread that came down from heaven.
Your ancestors ate manna and died,
but whoever feeds on this bread will live forever."

John 6:48–58 (NIV)

⁶⁶From this time many of his disciples turned back
and no longer followed him.   **John 6:66 (NIV)**

The passage above presents the strongest argument against those who speculate about what Jesus could or couldn't have done due to the historical or cultural limitations of His time. In this instance, He tells the Jews—who rigorously observe countless rules of ritual purity—that they must eat His flesh and drink His blood to attain eternal life, an idea that could not have been more shocking or outrageous at the time. This teaching led most of His followers to abandon Him.

So, is Christ truly present in the Eucharist?

If we approached this as scientists, limited to judging by observable phenomena, then based on what we see in Catholic churches, the 'real presence' appears to be a fact: A tangible sense of sacredness is present, as people are genuinely drawn together, forming a Holy Communion and striving to avoid sin and the delusion of righteousness to receive the Eucharist with proper reverence. These are all objective observations. Moreover, Jesus Himself affirms in the Gospels that these elements are integral to the heavenly reality He promised to those who love Him.

From a scientific perspective, we can say that Christ is truly present in the Eucharist to the same extent that consciousness exists in our neighbor: Both appear to be realities that cannot ever be—by design—figured out from *photons* or *atoms*. Why do many find it easier to make peace with the latter and not with the former? That, I do not know.

In conclusion, I see two plausible explanations for this reality. Either this is all a massive misunderstanding, with no true presence of God in churches or anywhere else—making everything in this book meaningless. Or, Christ's real presence is a profound reality in every Catholic church, where the Eucharist in the Tabernacle invites believers to spend time in silent adoration in proximity to the real Lord Jesus.

If the latter is true, the Lord Jesus remains truly and substantially present in His Church in a genuinely sacred way. If the former is true, the Church will gradually devolve into a mere folklore club, the priests into mere couches of happiness, and the people into well-catered creatures—possibly having all their physical needs met yet lacking the inherent dignity of those who eat Christ to become His true body, the most significant and direct instrument of divine Love in the universe.

Either everything is mere coincidence, or the Eucharist is the singular force that holds humanity in a more dignified order of being—where everything is at stake when Eucharistic reverence is diminished.

To a software designer, this may seem like a wonder—the Eucharist is so ingeniously designed that it is immediately evident it can never lead us astray. No sacred object stands in greater contrast to the man-made idols of sacred wells and golden calves. Furthermore, if this is true, what we witness during Catholic Mass appears, in a sense, to be an early attempt to bootstrap heaven on earth.

That said, it raises the question of whether humanity should attempt to bridge the gap between earthly and heavenly realities—and if so, to what extent. The 'internet,' for instance, can be seen as an early attempt to unite all living people into a single consciousness. Similarly, the coded reflection of the Logos I mentioned earlier would seek to imitate the true Logos in the mind of God.

Truthfully, I don't know what humanity is meant to achieve before the world ends with Christ's Second Coming. I can barely see one step ahead. What seems clear is that we cannot cultivate a unified consciousness of humanity through *infrastructures* like a dating site built in PHP, such as Facebook, or a service for broadcasting short text mobile messages like Twitter. And those are just the most absurd examples. Likewise, our understanding of the world cannot remain confined to mere phenomena—we cannot focus solely on actions and reactions while ignoring questions of meaning and purpose. We also cannot prioritize research of the external over the internal, nor can we limit our discoveries by expressing them in natural language.

This is what Joseph Ratzinger wrote on the subject in his book:

> The belief in the second coming of Jesus Christ and the fulfillment of the world in it can be understood as the conviction that our history is moving toward an Omega point—a mo-

ment in which it will become definitively clear and unmistakable that what appears to us as the stable, foundational reality is not merely unconscious, inert matter, but rather that the true, firm ground of reality is meaning. Meaning holds being together, gives it reality—indeed, meaning is reality. Being does not receive its foundation from below but from above.

We can already perceive, in a certain sense, this process of matter's integration into spirit and its transformation into a new form of unity in the reshaping of the world brought about by technology. The increasing manipulability of reality is beginning to blur the boundaries between nature and technology—so much so that the two can no longer be clearly distinguished. To be sure, this analogy is questionable in more than one respect. And yet, these developments hint at a world in which spirit and nature no longer stand merely side by side, but rather in which spirit integrates what seemed to be purely natural into itself, thereby creating a new world—a process that necessarily entails the passing away of the old one.

Of course, the end of the world in which Christians believe is something entirely different from the total victory of technology. But the merging of nature and spirit that takes place in this transformation allows us to grasp in a new way the direction in which the reality of faith in Christ's return is to be understood: Namely, as the belief in the ultimate unification of reality through the spirit.

I do not claim to know how humanity is meant to progress before the Second Coming of the Lord. I am uncertain how much of this is within our control as part of the divine plan for the 'new heaven' and 'new earth' mentioned in the book of Revelation. Beyond this, I have nothing more to add on the matter.

The Gospels present three distinct ways in which the Lord Jesus is present: First, in His mortal body when He lived among us; second, in the Eucharist; and third, in His resurrected, eternal 'new body,' which we have only glimpsed. This new body may prefigure the existence that awaits us after the resurrection of all at the end of time. The resurrected body was tangible yet existed in a different realm, allowing Him to move beyond physical constraints—appearing in different locations and vanishing instantly. This body radiated glory and majesty.

Catholic doctrine teaches that all people will be resurrected, including those who have rejected God. For the latter, it is daunting to imagine what their existence might entail. It is hard not to recall the illustrations from children's books that once provoked laughter. Not anymore. This world is full of unexpected and unsettling surprises.

I fear I have taken the very arc an evangelist should avoid at all cost—starting with Original Sin and ending with a vision of hell. I hope, however, that your overall impression was not that of a religion of fear, as Albert Einstein would put it.

At the very end, allow me to fix it by quoting the Creed in full:

> I believe in one God, the Father almighty,
> maker of heaven and earth,
> of all things visible and invisible.
>
> I believe in one Lord Jesus Christ,
> the Only Begotten Son of God,
> born of the Father before all ages.
> God from God, Light from Light,
> true God from true God,
> begotten, not made,
> consubstantial with the Father;
> through him all things were made.
> For us men and for our salvation
> he came down from heaven,
> and by the Holy Spirit
> was incarnate of the Virgin Mary,
> and became man.
> For our sake he was crucified
> under Pontius Pilate,
> he suffered death and was buried,
> and rose again on the third day
> in accordance with the Scriptures.

He ascended into heaven
and is seated at the right hand of the Father.
He will come again in glory
to judge the living and the dead
and his kingdom will have no end.

I believe in the Holy Spirit,
the Lord, the giver of life,
who proceeds from the Father and the Son,
who with the Father and the Son
is adored and glorified,
who has spoken through the prophets.

I believe in one, holy, catholic and apostolic Church.
I confess one Baptism for the forgiveness of sins
and I look forward to the resurrection of the dead
and the life of the world to come.

Amen.

— 20 —

The Age of Addiction

In the epilogue, I want to reflect on the implications of this book's message for our present reality in 2024. Until now, I have tried to present ideas as precisely as possible. However, in this chapter, I will relax that constraint somewhat, as some topics I am unable to discuss with precision.

Now that you are familiar with the core message—the Good News ('euangelion')—I find it acceptable to explore additional topics through analogies and simplifications. However, I do not think it is acceptable for all theology to devolve into mere vague approximations and poetic analogies, as this leads to a dumbed-down model of God—one that intelligent nonbelievers rightfully reject as inadequate, shallow, and flawed.

It is often said that God transforms every evil into an even greater good. I find this to be both an insightful and elegant observation. However, it is not a scientific statement—there is no unit to measure good or evil, nor a way to quantify and compare them. That said, while poetic language is not bound by the scientific method, it can still offer meaningful insights.

If we accept that the crucifixion of God is the worst act humanity could ever commit against its Creator—who chose to emerge from divine hiddenness and dwell among us—then it follows that God not only expected it but permitted it, solely because He intended to transform this event into a good so great that no other good could surpass it: "O certe necessarium Adae peccatum, quod Christi morte deletum est!"—"O truly necessary sin of Adam, which was blotted out by the death of Christ!" we sing in the Exultet.

140

This may sound like sharp logic, but in reality, it is not—it is not something that could be encoded in a programming language. And yet, on some level, I recognize its truth, and this realization deepens my appreciation for the profound nature of our condition.

By willingly enduring the most agonizing form of death, Christ Jesus revealed the true nature of our condition—one seen through the eyes of the godless villains we truly are. Few can bear such a perspective, yet it requires an extraordinary level of distortion to twist language into a narrative where this reality is not apparent.

Turning the other cheek is not merely an act of willingness to suffer evil at another's hands—it is a deliberate gesture designed to make villains see themselves as villains. It is like shining the light of truth on a reality tainted by Original Sin—Christ Himself is that light, as we recite in the Creed.

This force has demonstrated its power to bring empires to their knees, including, but not limited to, the Roman Empire with its empty customs. As a young student in London, Mahatma Gandhi recognized this force in the Gospels as a kind of 'spiritual dynamite'—one he would later wield to reshape history. Decades later, the same approach proved instrumental for John Paul II in helping to dismantle the evil Soviet Empire. If such power can work through human hands, what should we expect when wielded by God Himself, if not an effect magnified beyond measure?

This is why we must understand Love—the essence of God—not as mere metaphor, but as a real force, while recognizing the following as a poetic analogy—a conceptual shortcut shaped by ancient thought: I refer to the idea of God performing a mysterious and incomprehensible ritual—sacrificing His own Son to cleanse us from sin through His blood.

The true and operative force lies solely in the unconditional love of Christ, who willingly turned the other cheek and faced death out of love for us, that we might recognize our sinful condition and renounce it. We need not seek additional, unfathomable ritual mysteries to grasp the power at work—Love alone is the force that conquers evil. Anyone searching for an elusive mystical force behind the scenes is mistaken—to the point of idolatry.

Love is as physically potent in creation as dynamite is in destruction. This is a truth Christians must take literally—otherwise, they do not truly follow Christ.

To conform to God—to the Lord Jesus, the divine Logos—means being willing to suffer out of love for others, so that they may suffer less, expecting nothing in return but the joy of pleasing God. This is what naturally draws every heart, though many have yet to fully realize it.

12 "This is my commandment:
  That you love one another as I have loved you.
13   No one shows greater love
  than when he lays down his life for his friends.
14   You are my friends, if you do what I command you.
15   I don't call you servants anymore,
  because a servant doesn't know what his master is doing.
  But I've called you friends,
  because I've made known to you
  everything that I've heard from my Father."

John 15:12–15 (NIV)

This is why we honor firefighters, soldiers, missionaries, and all those who willingly embrace the possibility of suffering to save others.

Animals, lacking free will and thus incapable of rebelling against God, often endure great suffering—even unto death—so that other creatures, ultimately humans, may live. They seem to accept pain and suffering for the benefit of others.

Isn't it strange that evolution never produced ravens that poison wells with toxic berries to kill predators, nor birds that evolved strategies to attack humans, as in the famous horror story? There are countless possible survival strategies that God did not permit to evolve, and we should learn not only from what exists but also from what could have been—yet never came to be.

Animals may not love us, but God does—and He was willing to endure the same suffering, pain, and sacrifice they experience.

Does the immense physical suffering of animals make you tremble? Is this realization enough to turn you away from God? Why, then, do you celebrate a firefighter and his dog searching for people in the ruins after an earthquake? Conceptually, the firefighter made a decision for his dog similar to the one God made for His creatures. Why, then, do we celebrate one while recoiling at the other?

If sacrificing oneself unto death for one's friends is the pinnacle of love, then its apparent opposite—the ultimate abyss of evil—would be dehumanizing and killing another person to alleviate one's own suffering.

While we may hope that pleasing God and following His will ultimately lessens suffering in this broken world, making the elimination of suffering our highest goal will paradoxically lead to greater suffering in the long run. Why? Because this mindset fosters addiction.

The last century might rightly be called the Age of Addiction. In our quest to minimize suffering, we created immense moral hazards:

We became addicted to oil, funneling trillions to the world's evil overlords to ease the burdens of costly travel and goods transportation. Now, the very forces we bred by flooding them with easy money threaten humanity's very existence. They now kill us, even as we remain dependent on them—like addicts on their dealers. Moreover, we are now suffering the effects of extreme weather—consequences of the environmental damage our ancestors inflicted by burning the very substance they were addicted to.

Likewise, we have funneled trillions to oppressive rulers who exploit slave labor—all to shield ourselves from the hardship of costly goods. Now, these same overlords control essential industries—including pharmaceuticals—and will not hesitate to wield their power against us. Meanwhile, our own industries have collapsed, devastating communities and fueling substance abuse epidemics—all consequences of our shortsighted attempts to eliminate suffering without following God's will.

In the end, every hardship we seek to evade in defiance of God's will only deepen our suffering. Even the Church has not escaped unscathed. As a side effect of attempts to reduce it to the world's largest NGO tasked with eliminating suffering, true theology has been dismissed as overly complex and seemingly redundant. Through poor catechesis and dumbed-down theology, we may have risked leading countless souls—both believers and nonbelievers—toward eternal damnation by depriving them of the true image of God.

The coronavirus pandemic exposed these moral hazards—at the cost of millions of lives—yet we perceived it merely as a natural disaster filled with needless suffering. We changed little in production chains and continued to support criminal regimes. Yet this very example—the pandemic—could have demonstrated that there is no such thing as senseless suffering.

When confronted with suffering—suffering you neither chose nor can escape—you have a choice: You can suffer in defiance of God, or you can suffer with hope, trusting that your pain carries a meaning you may not yet perceive. This suffering—one that God, who suffers alongside you, has permitted—may serve to subtly redirect the course of our broken world, a world in which too many reject suffering and merely "kick the can down the road".

In Catholic tradition, entrusting one's suffering to God—believing in its hidden meaning—is known as 'offering up one's suffering.' And even the weakest, most exhausted soul retains the power to do this.

Every moment of suffering that we—or our ancestors—have evaded in defiance of God's will must eventually be repaid. Some may call this the wrath of God in an allegorical sense, yet no one considers broken legs or bruises—caused by ignorance of the laws of physics—as divine punishment. This principle remains consistent, regardless of which of God's laws one chooses to ignore.

If we refuse to embrace suffering out of love, future generations will inherit the burden we rejected. My generation confronts this reality in its rawest form. One can only hope that we choose to suffer with purpose, in union with God, rather than rebel against Him in anger and the despair of senseless suffering.

In this world, you have a choice: To suffer temporarily in your earthly life out of love for others, or to displace your suffering onto them—only to risk eternal suffering after death.

This also helps explain why Christ Jesus had to endure such an excruciating death. Had He been spared this suffering, it would imply that God Himself contradicted His own divine logic. It would suggest that we ought to resist suffering rather than embrace it when confronting evil with love. In such a case, even suicide might seem justifiable as a means to escape suffering. Likewise, one might justify euthanizing a suffering person out of misplaced mercy—believing that even God sought to evade suffering at His most agonizing moment.

If you choose to do evil, God's will shall still prevail—but at the cost of suffering. Otherwise, the kingdom of God would never come, and suffering would have no end. But if you choose to please God by embracing a share of suffering out of love for others, what remains for you to fear—either in this life or in the next?

As Joseph Ratzinger wrote:

> It is only through Him that one can act in a spirit of responsibility while at the same time being relaxed, joyful, and free, putting the things of this world at the service of redeeming love.

www.ingramcontent.com/pod-product-compliance
Lightning Source LLC
LaVergne TN
LVHW051241050326
832903LV00028B/2508